Gallito Pinto

Traditional Recipes from Costa Rica

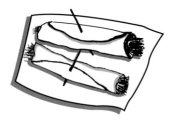

Gallito Pinto

Traditional Recipes from Costa Rica

Andrea Corrales

A Zona Tropical Publication
San Jose, Costa Rica

ISBN-978-0-9798804-8-3

Printed in China
10 9 8 7 6 5 4 3 2 1

Book design: Zona Creativa S.A.
Designer: Gabriela Wattson
Cover design and illustrations: Lacabeza estudio de diseño
Illustrator: Pili Aguirre
Editor and translator: Meg Mitchell

Published by Distribuidores Zona Tropical S.A.
www.zonatropical.net

Contents

Main Courses

Desserts and Treats for Coffee Hour

Temperature Chart

	FAHRENHEIT	CELSIUS
Very low	250-275	121-133
Low	300-325	149-163
Medium	350-375	177-190
Hot	400-425	204-218
Very hot	450-475	232-246
Extremely hot	500-525	260-274
Broil	550	287

Introduction

From Canada to Tierra del Fuego, food aficionados often say that Mexico and Peru are the only legitimate members of the club of great national cuisines in the Americas. Though pronouncements such as these are likely to cause grumbling from Argentina, Brazil, and, indeed, a host of other countries, it is true that the signature dishes from Mexico and Peru display a creativity, a delicacy of technique, a uniqueness—an exoticism even—found nowhere else in the Americas.

However, every country in the region—and Costa Rica in particular—produces a number of delicious dishes and ingredients. (An interesting aside: Many would argue that Costa Rica's version of the tamale is superior to that of Mexico.) And, if your tastes tend toward the tropical, then the abundant variety of tropical fruits used in Costa Rican recipes will surely please you.

Of course, this debate about food is very much a question of perspective. The simplicity of Costa Rican cooking, its reliance on tropical fruits, and the relative importance of legumes and tubers (as opposed to a gluttonous appetite for meat)—all this results in recipes that are healthy, unpretentious, and easy to prepare. Some of us prefer this approach to food to that of the gourmand's obsession for novelty and fancy techniques.

We hope that you'll have fun trying out the recipes in this book. We also hope that the recipes, illustrations, and cultural notes within will serve as a kind of introduction to Costa Rica, its people, and the rhythm of day-to-day life here.

Black Bean Soup /
Sopa negra
(6 - 8 servings)

Versions of black bean soup appear in Cuba, Colombia, Mexico, and throughout most of the rest of Latin America. This Costa Rican recipe does not call for the use of ham hock or other meat, so it counts as a vegetarian dish. Although black bean soup is generally served as an appetizer, Ticos in search of a light dinner will often dine on a bowl of this and nothing more.

Ingredients:

- 3 cups cooked black beans (see recipe on page 21).
- 3 cups water (use the soupy, rich water in which you cooked the beans; if needed, add fresh water to top off to 3 cups).
- salt (to taste).
- ½ bunch cilantro, finely chopped.
- 1 celery stalk, finely chopped.
- ½ red bell pepper, finely chopped.
- 1 medium onion.
- 4 eggs.

Preparation:

- Cook the black beans; drain off the water when finished (see suggestion above).
- Put beans and 3 cups water in a blender; purée until smooth. If the resulting mixture is too thick for your liking, strain off some of the remaining bean chunks.

- Transfer the blended beans and liquid to a large pot. Add salt, along with the cilantro, celery, bell pepper, and onion. Bring the soup to a boil and cook for about 3 minutes; stir frequently to prevent it from sticking to the pot.
- Break the eggs directly into the boiling soup; then immediately turn off the heat and cover the pot. The heat remaining in the pot will cook the eggs in just a few minutes.
- Garnish the soup with your garnish of choice. Some people like to add a dash or two of either Worcester sauce or Tobasco sauce.
- Serve hot with a side dish of white rice.

Cream of Ayote /
Crema de Ayote
(4 servings)

Ayote is a kind of squash that Costa Ricans use to prepare a range of dishes, including both cream of ayote and a sweet, dessert flan. (A winter squash such as butternut or cushaw, both commonly available outside of Costa Rica, are acceptable substitutes for ayote.)

This creamy soup makes a delicious, slightly sweet appetizer.

Ingredients:

- 3 lbs. ripe ayote or other winter squash. (The flesh of ripe ayote is a deep mustard-yellow color. Some supermarkets in Costa Rica make it easy to select ripe ayotes by

- 3 cups water for the soup.
- 1 cup heavy cream (or evaporated milk).
- 1 teaspoon of salt.

Preparation:

- Peel the squash and cut it into cubes. Place in a saucepan with just enough water to cover the squash; bring to a simmer and continue cooking for 20 minutes, or until very soft.
- Drain the cooked squash and transfer it to a blender; add 3 cups of water, heavy cream (or evaporated milk), and salt. Blend thoroughly.
- Strain the mixture and then simmer for 5 minutes, stirring constantly.
- Serve hot.

Cream of Pejibaye /
Crema de Pejibaye
(4 servings)

The pejibaye plam tree, which is native to the Americas, has been cultivated since early human civilization. Costa Ricans eat not only the pejibaye fruit, which has a distinctive nutty taste (it isn't at all sweet), but also heart of palm, which is produced from the inner core of the trunk. The pejibaye fruit is small, orange (sometimes reddish), and very nutritious. The flesh of the fruit has a somewhat chaulky consistency. It is never eaten raw but always first boiled, and then either served as an appetizer—sliced in half and topped with mayonnaise—or used to prepare this creamy soup.

Ingredients:

- 6 pejibayes: cooked, peeled, and cut into small pieces. (Many Costa Rican grocery stores sell cooked pejibayes.)
- 1 cup evaporated milk.
- 1 ½ cups milk.
- 1 can cream of chicken soup.
- 1 tablespoon of butter.
- ½ teaspoon of Complete Seasoning.
- salt (to taste).
- 1 tablespoon of fresh parsley, finely chopped.

Preparation:

- Boil the pejibayes in salted water (the fruit is sufficiently cooked when you can easily peirce its skin with a knife); peel the fruit and remove the single, large seed.
- Purée the pejibayes and the rest of the ingredients (except the parsley) in a blender or food processor until smooth; then strain.

- Simmer the mixture over medium heat for 10 minutes, stirring constantly to prevent lumps or sticking.
- Taste and add more salt as desired. Garnish with parsley and serve hot.

Tripe Soup / Sopa de mondongo
(6 - 8 servings)

As its name suggests, tripe (or *mondongo* in Spanish) is the key ingredient in this local dish. While some people are squeamish at the thought of eating tripe, this is a delicious soup, and one that also contains lots of vegetables and spices.

Ingredients:

- 3 lbs. tripe.
- 2 sprigs fresh rosemary.
- 2 sprigs fresh thyme.
- 1 teaspoon of salt.
- 1 tablespoon of Complete Seasoning.
- 2 tablespoons of Worcester sauce.
- 3 garlic cloves, minced.
- 1 celery stalk, chopped.
- 1 medium onion, quartered.
- 4 medium potatoes.
- 1 large sweet potato.
- 1 large, ripe chayote.
- 2 ripe ears of corn.
- 1 medium yuca.
- 1 large carrot.
- 1 large green plantain.

Preparation:

- Wash the tripe thoroughly; cut it into 2-inch squares. Place the tripe in a pot and add water sufficient to cover the meat.
- Add to the pot: rosemary, thyme, salt, Complete Seasoning, 1 tablespoon of Worcester sauce (save the other tablespoon for later), garlic, celery, and onion.
- Cook over medium heat until the tripe is tender (i.e., once it is easy to chew and has lost its tough consistency). In a regular pot, the tripe might take 2 to 2 ½ hours to cook; in a pressure cooker, the time is substantially reduced.
- While the tripe is cooking, peel the potatoes, sweet potato, chayote, corn, yuca, carrot, and plantain. Dice the vegetables into smallish cubes.
- Once the tripe is tender, add the diced vegetables and another tablespoon of Worcester sauce; pour in enough water to just barely cover all the ingredients.
- Simmer gently until the vegetables are tender, at which time the dish is ready. (Cooking tip: in this recipe, yuca is the vegetable with the longest cooking time. When it becomes tender, therefore, you know that the soup is done.)

Mealtimes

Costa Ricans—like people in many other countries around the world—generally eat three meals a day. Unlike in many European countries, however, meals in Costa Rican homes generally consist of a single course, except on more formal occasions—or in restaurants—where multiple courses are not uncommon. Ticos also customarily enjoy a mid-morning or mid-afternoon coffee break, at which coffee is almost always accompanied by some kind of bread or pastry (pound cake is very popular). For many people, these coffee breaks are something of a sacred ritual, and it is not uncommon to see a bankteller, precisely at the alloted time, hastily place a "closed" sign at his window, long lines of disgruntled customers notwithstanding.

The three regular meals are scheduled at widely varying times, depending on where people live and what they do for a living. In the countryside, for example, where people begin their workday at dawn, breakfast is eaten before 5 am, lunch before 11 am, and dinner before 4 pm. In cities, however, which is where the majority of Costa Ricans live, meals are eaten later in order to accomodate urban work schedules: in the public sector, the workday starts at 7 am, whereas private-sector employees usally begin work at either 8 am or 9 am. And people employed at retail stores usually start work at around 10 am. Breakfast is eaten between 6 am and 9 am (some people eat at work, taking advantage of the 15-minute coffee break that many employers provide). Lunch is eaten between noon and 2 pm, and dinner between 6 pm and 8 pm. Restaurants are usually open between 11 am and 11 pm, although they may close at some point during the day and reopen later.

It's difficult to overstate the importance of family in Costa Rican cultural life. Most families try to enjoy their meals together, whenever work and school schedules allow them to do so, and it's not uncommon for employees to drive from the workplace to home in order to eat lunch with their spouse and children.

Bocas

Barbudos

(4 servings)

This delicious dish is easy to make: you simply fry green beans in egg batter—and that's about it. *Barbudos*—there is no English word for this dish—literally means "the bearded ones," a name perhaps suggested by the appearance of the dish. In Costa Rica barbudos is a side dish eaten at both lunch and dinner.

Ingredients:

- 24 large green beans.
- 2 eggs, beaten.
- 1 tablespoon of flour.
- salt (to taste).
- vegetable oil.

Preparation:

- Cut the tips off the green beans and wash thoroughly. Add some salt to water, bring to a boil, and toss in the

green beans. Blanch only (remove the green beans as soon as they become tender).
- Place the beaten eggs in a small bowl. Add in the flour and salt while whisking to form a batter.
- In batches of six or so, dip the green beans into the batter.
- Pour the vegetable oil (just enough to prevent the green beans from sticking) into a large frying pan. Adjust heat to medium-high; when the oil is hot, slide the green beans into the frying pan and cook for about a minute, turning them so that they brown on both sides. (Keep in mind that the beans are already cooked, so they should be fried only long enough to cook the egg batter.)
- Serve hot.

Beans / Frijoles cocidos
(8 - 10 servings; about 4 to 5 cups)

Bean dishes—and rice dishes—are a staple of Costa Rican cuisine. They can be served as a side dish at either lunch or dinner, or they can be used to prepare other recipes such as refried beans and gallo pinto.

Ingredients:

- 1 lb. red or black beans (Costa Ricans generally prefer black beans).
- 2 celery stalks, finely chopped.
- 1 garlic clove, minced.
- 2 medium onions, finely chopped.
- 2 red bell peppers, finely chopped.

- ¾ cup cilantro, finely chopped.
- 6 fresh oregano leaves.
- salt (to taste).

Preparation:

- The night before preparing this dish, soak the beans in water, covering with two inches of water.
- Drain off the water and rinse the beans. Put the beans—and the celery, garlic, onions, bell peppers, cilantro, and oregano—in a pressure cooker or large pot. (If using a pressure cooker, add the salt at this point. If using a pot, add the salt only after the beans are cooked.)
- Add water (to the pressure cooker or pot), making sure to cover the ingredients with about 4 inches of water.
- If you're using a pressure cooker, cook over high heat until the pressure cooker emits steam; if you're cooking with a pot, place a lid on the pot and bring the water to a full boil.
- Lower the heat and continue cooking gently until the beans are tender. This should take about thirty minutes with a pressure cooker. It will take 1 to 1 ¼ hours with a regular pot (and you may need to add water occasionally so that the beans will continue to cook).

Cabbage Salad /
Ensalada de repollo
(6 - 8 servings)

This simple recipe is one of the most commonly served salads in Costa Rica. It is either eaten as a side dish or as one of the several items that make up a casado (see recipe on page 53).

(see recipe on page 53).

Ingredients:

- 1 large cabbage, chopped into thin strips about 3 inches long.
- 3 medium tomatoes, diced.
- 1 medium carrot, grated.
- 1 bunch of cilantro, finely chopped.
- vegetable oil.
- lime juice.
- pinch of salt.

Preparation:

- Place the chopped vegetables and the cilantro in a large bowl. Mix the ingredients together and add in the oil, lime juice, and salt.
- You can either serve the salad immediately or refrigerate and serve cold.

Ceviche
(8 servings)

Though Peru claims ceviche as its very own invention—and with persuasive evidence—there is lingering debate about the origin of this popular dish. It is a common item today on menus in a number of other Latin American countries, including Mexico, the countries of Central

America, Colombia, and Ecuador. Regional variatons abound, but nearly all recipes call for marinating raw fish or other kinds of seafood in citrus juice. In Costa Rica, particularly in the city of Puntarenas, ceviche is traditionally made with fish, though one innovative recipe calls for marinating green plantains in citrus juice—and dispensing with the fish altogether!

Ingredients:

- 2 lbs. fish fillets (sea bass, conger, sole, red snapper, or any similar soft-fleshed fish); make certain that all bones have been removed from the fish.
- ½ cup of each of the following ingredients (finely chopped): cilantro, onion, red bell pepper, and celery.
- 1 tablespoon of salt.
- 3 cups lime juice.

Preparation:

- Wash the fish thoroughly, then cut into bite-size pieces; place the fish in a glass bowl.
- Add the rest of the ingredients; the lime juice should completely cover the fish.
- Refrigerate and let marinate for 1 hour.

Ceviche can be served as soon as it has been marinated (it stays fresh for up to 2 days). Since fish has a tendency to go bad rather quickly, make sure to refrigerate between meals. Ceviche should be served slightly chilled. In Costa Rica, people like to place a small portion of ceviche on a soda cracker—and add a dab of ketchup, Tabasco sauce, or mayonnaise.

Chancletas de chayote

(6 servings)

Chancletas is the Costa Rican word for flip-flops. But nobody really knows—or seems to care for that matter—how this tasty dish, which is served as a side dish at both lunch and dinner, got its name. Though labeled a vegetable in the marletplace, chayote is actually a squash-like fruit, a substitute for which may be hard to find outside of Latin America (see p. 139 for suggestions).

Ingredients:

- 3 ripe chayotes.
- ¼ cup of butter (same as ½ stick).
- 1¾ cups of any mild, white cheese, grated.
- 1 tablespoon of sugar.
- ½ cup of raisins (optional).
- ½ tablespoon of vanilla (optional).
- ¼ cup of parmesan cheese, grated.
- 3 tablespoons of breadcrumbs.

Instructions:

- Preheat the oven to medium.
- Cut the chayotes in half, lengthwise.
- Place them in a pot with enough water to cover. Add salt and cook over medium heat for about 20 minutes—until the chayotes become soft.
- Drain the chayotes and allow them to cool. Use a spoon to remove all the pulp, taking care not to break the "shell" or skin. Set aside the pulp and skins and throw away the seeds.
- Mash the pulp with the butter, white cheese, and sugar (and raisins and vanilla if using).
- Using this mixture, stuff the chayote skins. Sprinkle parmesan cheese and breadcrumbs on top of each chayote.
- Bake the chancletas about 15 to 20 minutes—until they are golden brown.
- Serve hot.

Corn and Chayote Stew /
Guiso de chayote con elotes tiernos
(4 servings)

Corn and chayote, two of the most popular vegetables in Costa Rican cuisine, are combined in this simple recipe to prepare a delicious stew that can be served as an appetizer or vegetable side dish. This is fantastically easy to prepare!

Ingredients:

- 1 cup of ripe chayote (peeled and finely chopped).
- 1 garlic clove, minced.
- 1 small onion, finely chopped.
- 2 tablespoons of cilantro, finely chopped.
- 2 cups sweet corn (fresh or canned).
- ½ cup milk.
- 1 chicken-bouillon cube (better yet, 1 cup chicken broth).
- 1 tablespoon of butter.
- 1 teaspoon of sugar.
- pinch of fresh black pepper.

Preparation:

- Place the chayote along with the rest of the ingredients in a pot and simmer over medium heat until the vegetables are very tender.
- Serve hot.

Enyucados

(4 servings)

Enyucados are little balls—or rolls—of fried dough (made from yuca and cheese) that are filled with either meat or cheese. If you're new to the country, don't be surprised to find this dish served at just about any time of the day, from morning to late evening.

Ingredients:

- 2 lbs. yuca.
- salt (to taste).
- ½ small onion, finely chopped.
- ½ red bell pepper, finely chopped.
- 1 garlic clove, minced.
- ½ cup of any mild, white cheese.
- ¼ cup (½ stick) of butter, melted.
- breadcrumbs.

Ingredientes for the beef filling:

- ½ small onion, finely chopped.
- ½ red bell pepper, finely chopped.
- 1 tablespoon vegetable oil.
- ¼ lb. ground beef.
- salt and pepper (to taste).
- ½ tablespoon of Worcester sauce.

Note: Some people prefer to substitute grated cheese (of various kinds) for the meat filling.

Preparation:

- While the yuca is boiling (instructions below), make the beef filling. Over medium heat, sauté the onion and bell pepper in vegetable oil. Add the meat, salt, pepper, and Worcester sauce. Stir thoroughly and continue to sauté until beef is cooked through. Remove the sauté pan from the heat and allow the ingredients to cool. Set aside.

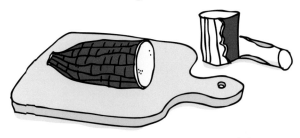

- Wash and peel the yuca; cut into 2-inch-long pieces. Place the yuca in a pot, cover with water, and add salt. Simmer over medium heat until the yuca softens (30-40 minutes).
- When the yuca is soft, remove from pot and drain off the water. Mash the yuca thoroughly with a large fork. Add the onion, pepper, garlic, and cheese—along with the butter—and mix well.
- Take a heaping tablespoon of the yuca dough, and place it on a piece of plastic wrap (a plastic bag will do). Flatten the dough into a rectangular shape; in the center of the dough, put a small amount of the meat filling (or grated cheese if you prefer). Roll the yuca around the filling, forming cylinders about an inch in diameter, and pinch the cylinder to seal it, making sure that the meat (or cheese) is completely wrapped within the dough. Prepare the rest of the yuca "balls."
- Roll each yuca ball in the breadcrumbs.
- Add enough oil to a frying pan to prevent the balls from sticking, and turn the heat to high. When the oil is hot, fry the balls, turning to brown them on all sides.
- Serve hot.

Escabeche

(6 - 8 servings)

The word *escabeche* refers to the process of marinating foods in oil and vinegar, and it is also used to describe the dishes obtained by this method. Costa Rican escabeche is made with vegetables and is served as both a side dish and a salad—at either lunch or dinner.

Ingredients:

- ⅓ cup vegetable oil.
- 4 garlic cloves, minced.
- 4 medium carrots, cut into thin strips.
- 2 cups water (¼ cup initially, then the remaining water).
- 1 medium cauliflower, cut into bite-sized florets.
- 1 ½ cups green beans, cut into 1-inch pieces.
- 1 ½ cups white vinegar.
- 2 medium onions, sliced into rings.
- 1 red bell pepper, cut into thin strips.
- 3 bay leaves.
- 4 oregano leaves.
- 4 clove-spice buds.
- 2 teaspoons of salt.

Preparation:

- Place the vegetable oil (over medium heat) in a pan, then sauté the garlic. Add the carrots and ¼ cup of water and cook for 5 minutes.
- Add the cauliflower and green beans and cook for another 5 minutes.
- Add the vinegar and the remaining water, along with the onions, bell pepper, bay leaves, oregano, clove spice, and salt. Cook over low heat (stirring occasionally) for approximately 1 hour, or until the vegetables are tender. Remove pan from the heat and set the ingredients aside to cool.
- Put the escabeche in a container and refrigerate. Serve cold.

Fried Plantains / Patacones
(4 servings)

Patacones are fried slices of ripe plantain. Originally of African origin, this dish is now popular in many Latin American countries. Regional names vary— in Nicaragua and Puerto Rico, for example, patacones are called tostones. Frequently served with a refried-beans dip, patacones make delicious snacks and appetizers. In Costa Rica, they are very popular in bars and restaurants.

Ingredients:

- 2 green (unripe) plantains.
- 1 teaspoon of salt.
- vegetable oil.

Preparation:

- Peel the plantains and cut them into circular slices approximately 1 inch thick.
- Into a heavy frying pan, pour about a half inch of oil. Heat the oil until very hot: to know if the oil is hot enough, drop a water droplet into the oil; the droplet should vaporize instantaneously.
- Fry the plantain slices until they take on a golden color.
- Place the fried slices on a chopping board and flatten each gently with a rolling pin or the bottom of a bottle or glass.
- Return the slices to the oil and refry until they become crisp and turn golden-brown.
- Drain the patacones on paper towels, sprinkle them with salt, and serve hot.

Note: Patacones are usually served with refried black beans (see recipe on page 38) or guacamole—or both— as a tasty dip.

Fried Yuca / Yuca frita

(4 servings)

The yuca that we eat (also called cassava) is the edible root of the yuca plant. Ancient peoples from regions of South America traveled north and introduced yuca here, where it became a staple of the pre-Columbian diet. Today, Costa Ricans continue to enjoy yuca and they use it to prepare all manner of local dishes.

Ingredients:

- 1 lb. yuca.
- water (to boil yuca).
- 2 chicken-bouillon cubes.
- 2 tablespoons of butter.
- 1 tablespoon of vegetable oil.
- 1 garlic clove, minced.
- salt (to taste).

Preparation:

- Wash and peel the yuca, then cut it crosswise into 3-inch-thick pieces.
- Add the water and the bouillon cubes to a large pot, and heat. When the water begins to boil, spoon the yuca into the water and cook until the yuca pieces are tender but before they begin to flake apart (about 30 minutes).
- Remove the yuca, place in a colander, and drain thoroughly.
- Cut each piece lengthwise, into 4 to 6 strips.
- Heat the butter and oil over medium-high heat, add the garlic, and fry for a couple of minutes. Add in the yuca pieces and fry until golden brown on all sides.

- Remove the yuca from the frying pan, dab off any excess oil, sprinkle with salt, and serve right away.

Note: In Costa Rica, a salsa rosada, made by mixing equal parts of mayonnaise and ketchup, is sometimes served as a dip for yuca.

Picadillo with Arracache (or Green Papaya) /
Picadillo de arracache o papaya verde
(6 - 8 servings)

Arracache is an indigenous word referring to an edible root that has played an important role in the food culture of various indigenous peoples of the Americas. As you're not likely to find arracache in either North American or European markets, you can substitute green (unripe) papaya for arracache in this recipe, with equally delicious—though noticeably different—results.

Ingredients:

- 1 lb. arracache (or unripe papaya), peeled and finely chopped.
- 2 tablespoons of onion, chopped.
- ⅓ red bell pepper, chopped.
- 2 tablespoons of celery, chopped.
- 1 garlic clove, minced.
- ½ teaspoon of achiote.

- 2 tablespoons of cilantro, chopped.
- ⅓ lb. ground beef.
- ¼ lb. chorizo sausage, either ground or sliced into tiny pieces.
- 1 teaspoon of Worcester sauce.
- salt (to taste).

Preparation:

- Place arracache (or papaya) in a pot with enough water to cover the arracache. Boil until the root—or papaya—becomes very soft. Remove pot from the heat and drain off the water thoroughly to prevent the arracache from turning mushy. Set aside.
- In a pan, sauté the onion, bell pepper, celery, garlic, achiote, and cilantro over medium heat until the ingredients begin to soften (note: there is no need to add oil). Add the ground beef, chorizo, and Worcester sauce and continue to cook until beef and chorizo are thoroughly cooked.
- Now add the arracache (or papaya) to the rest of the ingredients, mix well, and continue cooking until the arracache has reheated.
- Add salt, stir, and remove from heat.

Picadillo with Chayote, Sweet Corn, and Beef /
Picadillo de chayote, maíz dulce, y carne

(4 - 6 servings)

Chayote is a vegetable-like fruit that is native to Mexico and Central America. Costa Rican cooks use the stalk to make soup and other dishes; they use the fruit itself to make a variety of dishes, including this delicious picadillo.

Ingredients:

- 2 onions, chopped.
- 2 bell peppers, finely diced.
- 3 garlic cloves, minced.
- 1 lb. ground beef.
- 2 tablespoons of Worcester sauce.
- 2 tablespoons of Complete Seasoning.
- 2 beef-bouillon cubes dissolved in 1 cup of water.
- 2 ripe chayotes, peeled and chopped.
- 2 cups sweet corn.
- 1 celery stalk, chopped.
- 1 cup cilantro, chopped.
- vegetable oil.

Preparation:

- In a shallow layer of vegetable oil, sauté (over medium-high heat) the onion, bell pepper, and garlic until the ingredients become soft, then add the ground beef and mix well.

- After thoroughly mixing, add the Worcester sauce and the Complete Seasoning and then mix again.
- When the meat is cooked, add the bouillon-cube "broth," chayote, corn, celery, and cilantro—and stir.
- Cover, lower the heat to medium, and simmer until the chayote is completely tender.

Picadillo with Green Beans & Carrots / Picadillo de vainicas con zanahoria

(4 - 6 servings)

Put simply, picadillo is a generic term used to decribe any number of dishes made by mixing together an assortment of finely chopped up ingredients (in Spanish, *picar* means "to chop up"). Served as side dishes, picadillos are generally eaten with fresh, soft tortillas—at lunch and dinner. The number of distinct recipes for this dish are as various as you can imagine, and nearly everyone's grandmother claims her own special version.

Ingredients:

- 1 onion, chopped.
- ½ red bell pepper, chopped.
- 3 garlic cloves, minced.
- 1 celery stalk, chopped.
- ¾ cup cilantro, chopped.

- vegetable oil.
- 3 cups of green beans, chopped.
- 2 medium carrots, peeled and chopped.
- 1 beef-bouillon cube, dissolved in 1 cup water.
- Complete Seasoning (to taste).
- salt (to taste).

Preparation:

- Over medium heat, sauté (in a dash of vegetable oil) the following ingredients: onion, bell pepper, garlic, celery, and cilantro. Once the onion starts to turn a golden color, add in the green beans, carrots, and boullion-cube "broth." Stir ingredients continuously.
- Cook for a couple of minutes before spicing with Complete Seasoning. Turn heat to medium-high and continue coolking until most of the liquid evaporates.
- Taste, add salt as needed, and serve.

Note: You can also add ground beef to this picadillo recipe.

Refried Beans /
Frijoles molidos
(makes a dip that serves 6 - 8)

Refried beans are often served at restaurants, bars, parties, and social gatherings as a dip for tortilla chips. Some people like to add a dash of sugar, while others prefer to add Tabasco sauce—or both.

Ingredients:

- 2 cups cooked black beans (see recipe on page 21).
- 1 teaspoon of mustard.
- 1 teaspoon of olive oil.
- 1 teaspoon of sugar (optional).
- Tabasco sauce to taste (optional).
- ½ cup mozzarella or other mild cheese, grated (optional).

FRIJOLES

Preparation:

- Place the cooked beans—along with about a cup of the liquid they were cooked in—into a blender and purée until smooth. As the mixture is blending, add in the mustard, olive oil, and, if you like, sugar and/or Tabasco sauce.
- Pour the mixture into a large pan; simmer over low heat, stirring constantly to prevent it from sticking.
- When hot, serve the beans in a bowl and top with grated cheese.

Note: Serve with tortilla chips.

Ripe Plantains /
Plátanos maduros
(6 servings)

This dish—a sugary, gooey, delicious treat—is served more often as a side dish—at breakfast, lunch, and dinner—than as a dessert. At breakfast, ripe plantains often appear on the same plate alongside gallo pinto. When eaten for dessert, a generous portion of syrup is often heaped on top.

Ingredients:

- 3 very ripe plantains.
- vegetable oil (optional).

Ingredients for syrup (optional):

- ½ teaspoon of vanilla extract.
- 1 cup of sugar.
- cinnamon (to taste).
- 1 ½ cups of water.

Preparation:

- Peel the plantains and cut them into circular slices about a half-inch thick. Although plantains are traditionally fried in a small amount of vegetable oil, you can also cook them without oil if you use a non-stick pan. Either way, cook the plantains over medium heat until they turn a golden color. (Serve plain or with a dash of sugar on top.)

- To make a syrupy dessert: Place the fried plantain slices, vanilla extract, sugar, cinnamon, and water into a pan. Cook over low heat for approximately 15 minutes, or until the liquid has formed into a thick syrup. You can present the plantains and syrup in a dessert bowl or—if you want to serve a less syrupy dessert—remove the plantains from the syrup, place on a dessert plate, and then add a small amount of syrup on top.

Note: Whether you prepare the plantains with or without syrup, they are best served hot.

Ripe Plantains en Gloria /
Plátanos maduros en gloria
(6 servings)

This is yet another plantain dish that is extremely popular among Costa Ricas, who serve it both as a side dish and a dessert. As you plan your menu, keep in mind that this dish is very filling, and you might want to accompany it with a fairly light main course.

Ingredients:

- 3 very ripe plantains, fried.
- ¾ cup sugar.
- 1 ½ cups of mozzarella cheese, grated.
- ¾ cup milk.

Preparation:

- Preheat the oven to medium.
- Fry the plantains as in the previous recipe (minus the syrup).
- Select a casserole dish or other ovenproof glass container; grease the dish; place a layer of plantains over the surface of the dish—and sprinkle with sugar and a layer of cheese. Add another layer of plantains and repeat the process until you have used up all the ingredients. Finish by pouring the milk over the plantains.
- Bake for about 30 minutes (until the plantains look firm, but not dry).
- Serve hot.

Russian Salad /
Ensalada rusa
(4 servings)

Despite its name—and wherever this dish actually originated—Russian salad is very much a part of Costa Rica's culinary tradition. It is often served as one of the several items that make up a casado.

Ingredients:

- 1 large beet.
- 1 large potato.
- 1 large carrot.
- 2 eggs.

- 3 tablespoons of mayonnaise.
- salt (to taste).
- 3 teaspoons of cilantro, finely chopped.
- 1 small celery stalk, finely chopped.

Preparation:

- Scrub the vegetables thoroughly, but leave them unpeeled.
- Cook the beet in a pressure cooker for 30 minutes (if using a regular pot, cook for approximately 1 hour). When the beet is finished cooking, set it aside to let cool.
- Place the potato, carrot, and eggs (in their shells) in a pot with enough water to cover the ingredients. Bring the water to a boil, and then reduce the heat; simmer for approximately 20 minutes. When finished cooking, allow the vegetables and eggs to cool.
- Using a spoon as a scraper, peel the beet, potato, and carrot (once they are cooked, it is very easy to remove their skins in this way). Chop the vegetables into small squares and mix them together in a large bowl.
- Peel the hard-boiled eggs. Cut the eggs in half; separate the yolks and store them for use in other dishes. Chop the whites into small pieces and add them to the other cooked ingredients.
- Add the mayonnaise, salt, cilantro, and celery to the cooked ingredients. Mix thoroughly.
- The salad can be served immediately, or, if you like, refrigerate it before serving.

Shell Pasta Salad with Tuna/

Ensalada de caracolitos con atún

(6 - 8 servings)

Costa Ricans generally serve this tasty, cold salad—often along with a serving of rice and beans—on the same plate as the main course.

Ingredients:

- 3 cups shell pasta.
- 1 tablespoon of vegetable oil.
- pinch of salt.
- 2 cans of tuna (6 ½ oz. each), drained.
- 1 cup of mayonnaise.
- 2 tablespoons of cilantro, chopped.
- 1 medium onion, chopped.
- 1 tablespoon of celery, chopped.
- 1 tablespoon of mustard.
- lime juice (1 medium lime).

Preparation:

- Add the vegetable oil and salt to a pot of water. Bring the water to a boil and cook the pasta until it is al dente—tender but firm. Drain the pasta and place it in a large bowl.
- Add the following ingredients to the bowl of pasta: tuna, mayonnaise, cilantro, onion, celery, mustard, and lime juice. Mix well.
- Refrigerate the salad and serve cold.

Variations on the above recipe call for adding sweet corn, green peas, or Worcester sauce (or some combination of the three).

Taco Tico
(6 - 8 servings)

Costa Rica's version of the taco (a Spanish word that means wedge) is very similar to one of the many recipes that come from Mexico. In this country, it consists of a fried corn tortilla stuffed with meat, shredded cabbage, and a mild sauce.

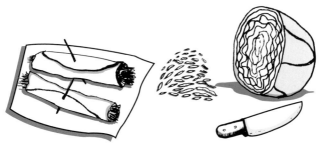

Ingredients:

- 1 small cabbage, finely chopped.
- salt (to taste).
- ½ cup of ketchup.
- ½ cup of mayonnaise.
- ½ tablespoon of Worcester sauce.
- 1 tablespoon of mustard.
- 20 medium-sized corn tortillas.
- 1 lb. beef (or pork), cooked and shredded.
- vegetable oil for frying.

Note: Make sure you have toothpicks and paper towels on hand before you start preparing this dish.

Preparation:

- Finely chop the cabbage, sprinkle with a little salt, and set it aside.
- In a small bowl, mix togther the ketchup, mayonnaise, Worcester sauce, and mustard. Set this sauce aside for later use.
- Scoop a small portion of meat into the tortilla; roll up the tortilla and secure it with a toothpick. Prepare the rest of the tacos in like manner.
- Coat the bottom of a heavy frying pan with vegetable oil. Place the pan over high heat; when the oil is near sizzling hot, fry the tacos (in batches of five or six) until a golden color.
- Remove the tacos from the pan and set them on paper towels to drain absorb excess oil.
- Remove the toothpick; open the tortilla; stuff a small portion of the cabbage and the sauce to the taco, and refold it.
- Serve immediately.

Tortillas

(Makes about 15 tortillas 5-inches in diameter)

Tortillas play a vital role in the culinary heritage of peoples throughout the Americas. How they are made—and how they are eaten—varies widely from region to region—often even within the same country. In Costa Rica, the standard tortilla is small and thin and may be served with breakfast, lunch, or dinner. While in the past the making of tortillas was a household activity, nowadays most people buy tortillas at the grocery store—and as a result miss out on the wonderful smell and taste of homemade tortillas.

Ingredients:

- 2 cups corn flour.
- 1 ¼ cups water.
- salt (to taste).

Preparation:

- Place the corn flour in a deep bowl. (Also add a pinch of salt, if you like.) Gradually pour in water while kneading the resulting doughy mass. Knead until the dough is smooth and no longer has a sticky texture.
- To make a tortilla, take a dollop of dough and roll it into a ball about 1 ½ inches in diameter. Place the ball on a sheet of cling wrap or waxed paper and place another sheet on top. Flatten the ball using a plate or a pan; remove the top sheet of cling wrap and spread out the tortilla with your fingers until it is about 5 inches wide, trying to give it an even shape. (You can, of course, also use a tortilla press.)
- Fry the tortillas in a pan with a little vegetable oil, or cook them without any oil in a nonstick pan. Flip once to ensure that each side is well cooked.

White Rice / Arroz blanco
(4 - 6 servings)

Costa Ricans very seldom eat a meal that doesn't include rice. Often a side dish, rice is also a key ingredient in a wide variety of dishes, including recipes that call for adding chicken, pork, or heart of palm. Rice is even used to prepare desserts, most commonly rice pudding. In Costa Rica, white rice is rarely served plain—even when a side dish—and the following recipe is fairly typical in that it calls for adding a number of ingredients to "white rice."

Ingredients:

- 3 tablespoons of vegetable oil.
- 1 celery stalk, finely chopped.
- 1 medium onion, finely chopped.
- ½ red bell pepper, finely chopped.
- 5 garlic cloves, minced.
- 2 cups rice (rinsed and drained).
- 3 cups hot water.
- 1 ½ teaspoons of salt.

Preparation:

- Place the oil in a pot and heat (over a medium flame).
- Add the celery, onion, and bell pepper to the oil and sauté until a golden color. Then add the garlic and cook for another minute. Next, add in the rice and stir the entire mixture for a couple of minutes—until the rice is a slightly golden hue.
- Add the hot water and salt and bring to a boil. Reduce heat to low, cover the pot, and cook until the rice absorbs the water completely (about 20 minutes).
- When the rice is done, remove the pot from the stove. Stir before serving.

"Bocas" and "Gallos"

Salchichón

In Costa Rica and Nicaragua, appetizers at parties and other social gatherings are called bocas (appropriately enough, *boca* is the Spanish word for mouth). In Spain, the corresponding word is *tapa*, while the words *botana* and *pasaboca* are equivalent words used in other Spanish-speaking countries.

The most popular traditional bocas include patacones, ceviche, the taco tico, fried yuca, and refried beans with tortilla chips. And non-traditional snacks like nachos with cheese are increasingly common today.

At many bars and restaurants, especially those that appeal to the common folk, bocas are generally the least expensive item on the menu. In fact, it used to be customary to serve a free boca with each beer, but, sadly, fewer and fewer places now do this.

Among the most common bocas are gallos. Gallos are heated corn tortillas served with meat, cheese, refried beans, and any number of other toppings. Eating a gallo is a bit of an art: You scoop the filling of your choice into the middle of the tortilla, fold it in half like a soft taco, and eat it with your fingers.

Gallos are so popular that they have transcended their status as an appetizer, and are a staple of home cooking. At lunch or dinner, the main course and side dishes may be served with tortillas and eaten in gallo fashion.

main
courses

Casado

(4 servings)

The casado, which is not a specific recipe but a way of serving a constellation of dishes for lunch, is very much a defining feature of daily life in Costa Rica. The word *casado* means "married," and, indeed, its very sound connotes a soft-focus view of family, hearth, and home. Although many restaurants offer the option of a vegetarian casado, the standard plate includes a piece of meat (beef, pork, chicken, or fish), rice and beans, a salad, picadillo, and fried, syrupy-sweet plantains. All these components are piled high on the same plate—so juices mix and spread—and those on a diet might as well resign themselves to temporary defeat.

Ingredients:

- 2 cups of white rice (see recipe on p. 48).
- 2 cups of cooked beans (see recipe on p. 21).
- 4 servings of salad (see salad recipes on pp. 42-44).
- 4 servings of picadillo (see picadillo recipes on pp. 34-37).
- 4 servings of fish, chicken, pork, or beef (steak with onion is particularly popular; see recipe on p. 67).
- 4 servings of plantains en gloria (see recipe on p. 41).

Preparation:

- On a plate place a smallish portion of each of the following: rice, beans, salad, and picadillo, along with 1 serving of beef, chicken, or fish, and three or four pieces of plantain.
- Serve hot.

Chickpeas with Pork /
Garbanzos con cerdo
(6 - 8 servings)

This dish is yet another variant on the rice and pork theme. Here, chickpeas replace the rice; throw in spices and some other ingredients and the result is a hearty, healthy main course.

Ingredients:

- vegetable oil.
- 2 small onions, chopped.
- 1 bell pepper, chopped.
- ¾ cup celery, finely chopped.
- 5 garlic cloves, minced.
- 3 cups boneless pork loin, cut into small pieces.
- 2 tomatoes, peeled, seeded, and crushed.
- 1 teaspoon of dried thyme.
- salt (to taste).
- 1 teaspoon of dried oregano.
- ½ cup cilantro, chopped.
- 3 cups cooked chickpeas (also know as garbanzos).

Preparation:

- Place a dash of vegetable oil in a large pot; over medium heat, sauté the onion, bell pepper, and celery. When the ingredients start to brown, add the garlic, pork, tomatoes, thyme, salt, oregano, and cilantro.
- Cover the pot and let it simmer over low heat until the meat is tender and cooked through.
- Add the chickpeas, stir well, and continue to cook for 10 minutes to allow flavors to combine.

Gallo Pinto

(4 - 6 servings)

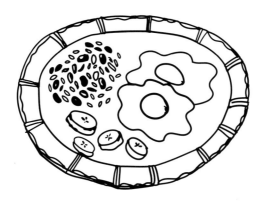

Costa Rica's quintessential national dish is very much a reflection of the country's multi-ethnic soul. In essence, it is a mixture of rice, which was brought over by the Spaniards, and beans, a crop cultivated by early indigenous peoples, and later, by Afro-Caribbean immigrants. If you avoid the recipes that call for throwing in a heaping mound of lard, you'll end up with a tasty, healthy meal.

Ingredients:

- 1 tablespoon of butter.
- 1 teaspoon of red bell pepper, finely chopped.
- 2 tablespoons of onion, finely chopped.
- 2 tablespoons of cilantro, finely chopped.
- powdered garlic (to taste).
- 2 cups cooked beans (see recipe on page 21).
- 1 tablespoon of Worcester sauce.
- ½ teaspoon of ground cumin.
- 2 cups cooked rice (see recipe on page 48).

Preparation:

- In a large saucepan, melt the butter over medium heat. Add in the bell pepper, onion, cilantro, and garlic—and cook until the vegetables begin to soften.
- Add the beans, Worcester sauce, and cumin. Stir thoroughly and allow to simmer for about 2 minutes. Mix in the rice, stir well, and continue to cook for another 3 minutes.
- Remove from heat and stir again before serving.

Note: In tradition-bound homes, gallo pinto is served at breakfast, often with a dollop of sour creme on top, but it's not uncommon to see late-night revellers eating a plate of gallo pinto at 2:00 am to stave off next-day jitters.

Olla de Carne
(8 - 10 servings)

This and gallo pinto are perhaps Costa Rica's two most signature dishes. Olla de carne, liberally translated as "a meat-filled pot," is a very hearty soup made with beef and various kinds of vegetables. It is so hearty, in fact, that it is generally served as a main course rather than an appetizer.

This soup is said to have originated in Spain, but—whether true or not—the incorporation of local vegetables into the dish has made it a decidely Costa Rican affair.

Ingredients:

- 2 lbs. beef (stew meat), cut into 1-inch pieces.
- 5 cups water.
- 3 garlic cloves, minced.
- 2 celery stalks, chopped.
- 1 bunch of cilantro, chopped.
- 1 medium onion, chopped.
- 1 red bell pepper (small), chopped.
- salt (to taste).
- 1 large carrot.
- 2 ears of corn.
- 1 ripe chayote.
- 1 lb. yuca.
- 1 lb. ripe ayote (can substitute winter squash).
- 1 lb. sweet potatoes.
- 2 plantains (one nearly ripe, the other still green).
- 4 potatoes.

Preparation:

- In a large pot, combine the beef, water, garlic, celery, cilantro, onion, bell pepper, and salt. Cook over low heat (don't allow the liquid to come to a boil) for approximately one hour, stirring frequently, until the broth becomes dark.
- Now that the broth is dark, increase the heat to high and bring the liquid to a boil. Cook for another 10 to 15 minutes (or until meat is tender), continuing to stir.
- Peel the remaining vegetables—carrots, corn, chayote, yuca, ayote, sweet potatoes, plantains, and potatoes— and cut them into 2-inch pieces.
- Add the vegetables to the meat and broth. Start with vegetables that require a longer cooking time (carrots, corn, chayote, plantains) and a few minutes later add the others (yuca, ayote, sweet potatoes, potatoes). Cook until tender.
- Taste and correct for salt.

Note: The vegetables may be served separately from the the meat and broth, though more commonly the entire concoction is served together in a soup bowl. Olla de carne is nearly always accompanied with a side dish of rice.

Potatoes with Chorizo /
Papas con chorizo
(6 - 8 servings)

This delicious traditional stew is served as a main course.

Ingredients:

- 8 medium potatoes, peeled and diced.
- 1 tablespoon of salt.
- 3 chorizo sausages (or other kind of spicy sausage).
- 1 medium red bell pepper, finely chopped.
- 2 garlic cloves, minced.
- 1 sprig of cilantro, chopped.
- 1 medium onion, finely chopped.
- 1 tablespoon of Complete Seasoning.
- 1 teaspoon of achiote.
- 2 tablespoons of Worcester sauce.

Preparation:

- Place the potatoes in a pot with enough water to cover them; add salt and boil until the potatoes are soft—not so soft that they begin to fall apart, but you should be able to easily insert a knife into them.
- While the potatoes cook, heat an ungreased frying pan over medium heat. Remove the casings from the sausages and fry them, using a wooden spoon to break up the sausages into small pieces.
- Add to the frying sausages the rest of the ingredients: bell pepper, garlic, cilantro, onion, Complete Seasoning, achiote, and one tablespoon of Worcester sauce. Continue cooking over medium heat, stirring every now and then to prevent the ingredients from sticking.
- When the potatoes are done, discard ¾ of the water remaining in the pot; add in the sausages and other ingredients—and one more tablespoon of Worcester sauce.
- Partially cover the pot and continue to simmer over low heat—stirring occasionally—until the potatoes are completely soft.

Pozol

(6 - 8 servings)

Although pozol stew is much more popular in Mexico than in Costa Rica, it is still a popular dish here, both at lunch and at dinner. The key ingredient is hominy, a specially processed form of corn.

Ingredients:

- 2 tablespoons of vegetable oil.
- 1 lb. boneless pork, cut into small squares.
- ½ lb. pre-roasted pork ribs, each cut in half.
- 1 onion, finely chopped.
- 1 red bell pepper, finely chopped.
- 2 garlic cloves, minced.
- 1 tablespoon of dried oregano.
- salt and pepper (to taste).
- 2 tomatoes, chopped.
- 3 cans (15 oz.) of hominy, drained and rinsed.
- 1 bunch of cilantro, chopped.
- 1 tablespoon of Worcester sauce.

Preparation:

- Heat the vegetable oil in a large pot over medium heat and sauté the pork and ribs, along with the onion, bell pepper, garlic, oregano, salt, and pepper. Add the tomatoes and cook until the vegetables are tender and the pork is cooked through.
- Add the hominy and lower the heat. Next add the cilantro and Worcester sauce, and continue to cook for 15-20 minutes, stirring every now and then. It's ready

to serve when the hominy is hot and the flavors are well blended.
- Serve hot in a deep bowl or tureen.

Note: Some people prefer to eat pozol the day after it is cooked, as the stew becomes thicker and the flavors seem to intensify. To vary this recipe somewhat, you can also add small pieces of green plantain or yuca.

Rice with Chicken /
Arroz con Pollo
(6 - 8 servings)

Rice with chicken—along with gallo pinto—is probably the most popular dish in Costa Rica. For an authentic Tico presentation, serve this dish with potato chips (sounds odd, but try it).

Ingredients:

- 2 large chicken breasts (deboned, skinless).
- salt (to taste).
- Worcester sauce.
- Complete Seasoning.
- 3 cups of rice.
- 1 teaspoon of achiote.
- ¼ cup (½ stick) butter (optional).
- 2 medium tomatoes.
- ½ cup cilantro, finely chopped.

- 1 medium onion, finely chopped.
- 1 celery stalk, finely chopped.
- ½ red bell pepper, finely chopped.
- minced garlic (to taste).
- 1 can of mixed carrots and peas (8 oz.). Use fresh vegetables, of course, if you have the time.

Preparation:

- Cut the chicken into 1-inch pieces. Poach the chicken in a little water—with salt (or Worcester sauce) and Complete Seasoning (to taste)—until it is cooked through. (Save the chicken broth to use to cook the rice in.)

- Cook the rice in a mixture of the chicken broth (add water if necessary), achiote, and butter (if desired). Make sure not to overcook the rice, as it should be slightly hard.
- Purée the tomatoes in a blender; in a large saucepan, combine the tomatoes, cilantro, onion, celery, and bell pepper. Add 2 teaspoons of Complete Seasoning, 3 tablespoons of Worcester sauce, and the garlic and salt. Stir well and place over low heat.
- Now add to the sauce the cooked chicken and the can of carrots and peas; next, add the rice (do not stir). Cover the pot and cook over very low heat for about 5 minutes, until the rice is tender.
- To produce a moister version of this dish, uncover the pan, stir, and serve immediately. (If you'd rather serve a slightly drier arroz con pollo, uncover the pan and cook a few minutes longer, then stir and serve.)

Rice with Heart of Palm /
Arroz con palmito
(4 - 6 servings)

Heart of palm, called *palmito* in Spanish, is a white and cylindrical vegetable that comes from the inner core of several palm-tree species. It is most often used in salads (sliced raw) and in this dish (in cooked form). Rice with heart of palm—a more refined and expensive alternative to rice with chicken, and just as popular at parties—is a delicious local dish.

Ingredients:

- 2 cups of rice.
- 3 cups chicken broth.
- 1 can cream of mushroom soup.
- ½ cup milk.
- ½ cup evaporated milk.
- 1 tablespoon of melted butter.
- 1 tablespoon of Complete Seasoning.
- 2 cans of heart of palm (14 oz. each).
- ½ cup mild cheese, grated (optional).

Preparation:

- Prepare the rice according to the recipe on p. 48, substituting chicken broth for water. Set aside.
- Preheat the oven to medium.
- In a blender, combine the cream of mushroom soup with the milk, evaporated milk, melted butter, and Complete Seasoning: purée.
- Transfer the mixture to a pot and simmer it over medium heat, stirring constantly until the ingredients thicken a little. Add the hearts of palm, mix well, and remove the pot from the stove.

There are two options for finishing the dish:

1. Add the cooked rice to the sauce and hearts of palm, mix well, and pour into an ovenproof baking dish, or:
2. To an ovenproof baking dish, pour in a layer of the sauce and hearts of palm; place a layer of rice over the sauce; alternate with layers, finishing with a layer of sauce and hearts of palm.

With either option, finish by sprinkling the grated cheese over the top (optional); cover the baking dish with foil, and bake for 20 minutes. Serve hot.

Rice and Pork /
Arroz con chancho
(6 servings)

In Costa Rican cooking, pork is a meat favorite of many a chef. Cash conscious homes often "stretch" the pork by adding it to stews and rice dishes, resulting in filling—and tasty dishes. One of the most popular is rice and pork; with just 1 lb. of the white meat, this dish can serve 6 people.

Ingredients:

- 2 cups of rice.
- 3 cups of water.
- 1 ½ teaspoons of salt.
- 1 tablespoon of vegetable oil.
- 1 teaspoon of achiote.
- 1 lb. of pork (pre-roasted and cut into small squares).
- 1 red bell pepper, chopped.
- 1 medium onion, chopped.
- 1 medium celery stalk, chopped.
- 3 large garlic cloves, minced.
- 1 cilantro sprig.
- 2 tablespoons of Worcester sauce.
- 1 tablespoon of Complete Seasoning.

Preparation:

- Cook the rice in a mixture of water, salt, vegetable oil, and achiote. Simmer until the water has evaporated to just below the surface of the rice.

- At this point, add the chopped pork, vegetables, and garlic and cilantro (do not stir). Add the Worcester sauce and the Complete Seasoning.
- Cover and and cook until the rice is tender. Stir well and serve.

Seasoned Beef Patties /
Tortas de carne
(4 servings)

These tasty meat patties—eaten at lunch or dinner—are invariably served with a side dish or two.

Ingredients:

- 1 lb. ground beef.
- 1 raw egg.
- 2 tablespoons of corn tortilla flour.
- 2 beef bouillon cubes, crushed.
- 1 teaspoon of Worcester sauce.
- ½ cup of onion, finely chopped.
- 2 tablespoons of cilantro, finely chopped.
- 2 garlic cloves, finely chopped.
- 1 red bell pepper, finely chopped.
- Complete Seasoning (to taste).

Preparation:

- Place the ground beef in a glass mixing bowl; mix in the egg, flour, and the other ingredients (in no particular order). Mix thoroughly.
- Form the mixture into 4 patties, each about 4 ½ inches in diameter.
- Over medium heat, cook the patties on a lightly-oiled griddle, turning once, until done to your liking.

Note: If there are any raw patties left over, you can store them; wrap in cling wrap to prevent the patties from sticking together, and then freeze.

Steak with Onion /
Bistec encebollado
(4 servings)

Steak with onion is perhaps the most popular beef dish in Costa Rica. In fact, it's very common here to include steak as the main item of the traditional casado dish (see description on page 53).

Ingredients:

- 4 steaks (about 5 ounces each—roughly the size of an extended hand and no more that ½ inch thick).
- 4 teaspoons of Worcester sauce (one teaspoon per steak).
- 2 teaspoons of Complete Seasoning (½ teaspoon per steak).

- vegetable oil.
- 1 tablespoon of butter.
- 2 medium onions, sliced into thin rings.
- 1 large garlic clove, minced.

Preparation:

- Place the steaks on a chopping board. (If the meat is tough, soften the steaks with a meat hammer.)
- Spread 1 teaspoon of Worcester sauce and ½ teaspoon of Complete Seasoning evenly on both sides of the steak.
- Pour some oil into a large frying pan, and turn the heat to medium. Melt the butter and then sauté the onions and minced garlic until golden brown.
- Remove the onion and garlic from the pan and set aside.
- In the same pan, fry the steaks. Once one side of the steak is cooked to your liking, flip it over and throw in some of the onions and garlic; finish cooking the steak.
- Serve each steak with some of the onions as topping.

Stewed Beef /
Carne mechada
(6 servings)

In Cost Rica, this dish is served in a number of ways. It is often served as the main dish (frequently along with rice or potatotes) at lunch or dinner; or, when wrapped in a tortilla, it makes a delicious gallo (to learn about gallos, see pp. 50-51); carne mechada can also be used as the key ingredient in a taco tico (see recipe on page 45).

Ingredients:

- 2 lbs. of stew meat.
- salt (to taste).
- rosemary, fresh or dried (to taste).
- Worcester sauce (to taste).

Ingredients for the sauce:

- 8 medium tomatoes.
- 1 tablespoon of salt.
- 1 tablespoon of olive oil.
- 3 garlic cloves, peeled.
- 4 large bay leaves.

Preparation:

- Place the meat, salt, rosemary, and Worcester sauce in a pot with enough water to cover the ingredients. Simmer over medium heat until the meat is very tender (about 3 hours), adding more water if necessary.
- While the meat is cooking: Purée the tomatoes, salt, olive oil, and garlic in a food processor or blender—there's no need to add water. Transfer to a pot, throw in the bay leaves, and simmer the mixuture for a few minutes.
- When the meat is done, remove from the pot; allow it to cool slightly, and then shred or cut the meat into thin strips. Finally, add the meat to the sauce and cook over low heat for 15 minutes—enough time to allow the flavors to combine.

Tongue in Sauce /
Lengua en salsa
(6 - 8 servings)

While tongue is not everyone's notion of culinary delight, this dish—a very popular one throughout Costa Rica—is usually served with a salad and either rice, pasta, or potatoes.

Ingredients:

- 1 beef tongue.
- salt (to taste).
- 2 tablespoons of dried rosemary.
- 4 medium tomatoes.
- 1 tablespoon of extra-virgin olive oil.
- 2 large garlic cloves, peeled.
- 5 sprigs of thyme.
- Complete Seasoning (to taste).
- ¼ cup red wine (optional).

Preparation:

- Wash the tongue thoroughly and cut off the ganglions that are located on the lower surface, near the base of the tongue.
- Over medium heat, boil the tongue in water (with salt and rosemary) until tender (about 3 hours). (When you can insert a knife through the tongue, then you know it's done.)
- Remove the tongue from the water; peel off its coarse outer skin, and cut into slices.

- To make the sauce, purée the tomatoes, olive oil, garlic cloves, and salt in a food processor or blender. Next, add the thyme and the Complete Seasoning and transfer the sauce to a pot. Heat the sauce (over medium heat) until foam begins to form on the surface; continue cooking until the foam disappears—at which point add in the tongue (and red wine, if using).
- Simmer over low heat until the tongue is heated through and the flavors have combined.

Tripe in Tomato Sauce /
Mondongo en salsa
(6 - 8 servings)

Tripe in tomato sauce is a favorite traditional dish in Costa Rica. It can be made with either pork or beef tripe. For the uninitiated, tripe is a meat that comes from the intestines and rubbery lining of the stomach—and if your appetite is still intact (or you're in an adventurous mood), then read on.

Ingredients:

- 3 lbs. tripe.
- 3 garlic cloves, peeled.
- 2 sprigs of rosemary.
- 2 sprigs of thyme.
- 1 tablespoon of salt.
- 1 medium onion, whole.

Ingredients for the sauce:

- 6 medium tomatoes, quartered.
- 2 garlic cloves.
- 1 tablespoon of olive oil.
- 1 tablespoon of salt.
- 4 bay leaves.
- 1 sprig of rosemary.
- 1 sprig of thyme.
- 1 tablespoon of Worcester sauce.
- 1 tablespoon of Complete Seasoning.
- 1 medium can of peas (8 oz.).

Preparation:

- Wash the tripe thoroughly and cut into 2-inch squares. Place the tripe in a pot (preferably a pressure cooker, to save time) with enough water to cover it, and add the garlic, rosemary, thyme, salt, and onion.
- Cook over medium heat until the tripe is tender (when it is easy to chew). In a regular pot, this may take 2-2 ½ hours, substantially less in a pressure cooker.
- While the tripe is cooking, make the sauce. Purée the tomatoes, garlic, olive oil, and salt in a food processer or blender.
- In a large pot, combine the sauce with the bay leaves, rosemary, thyme, Worcester sauce, and Complete Seasoning. Partially cover the pot and bring the sauce to a boil. Add the peas, then reduce the heat.
- Discard the water in which the tripe was cooked and add the meat to the sauce. Simmer for about 20 minutes, keeping the pot partially covered.
- Taste and correct for seasoning.

Vigorón
(8 - 10 servings)

Vigorón is a hearty, filling meal that includes pork, vegetables, and yuca. Fried pork and pork rind, called *chicharrón* when served separately, is a popular accompaniment to beer and Sunday afternoon soccer-watching.

Ingredients:

- 2 lbs. of yuca.
- 2 lbs. of cooked boneless pork, cut in 1-inch cubes (or you can mix 1 lb. of the pork with 1 lb. of fried pork rinds, each bite-size).
- 2 lbs. tomatoes, diced.
- 2 bunches of cilantro, chopped.
- ½ red bell pepper, chopped.
- 1 small onion, chopped.
- vinegar and salt (to taste).
- 1 large cabbage, finely chopped.
- 10 limes, quartered.

Preparation:

- Wash and peel the yuca. Cut it into 2-inch-long pieces and boil in lots of water until tender (yuca tends to aborb water). Drain the yuca, let it cool, and cut it into 1-inch squares.
- Cook the pork, drain, and set aside.
- In a small bowl, mix the diced tomatoes with the cilantro, bell pepper, onion, vinegar, and salt.
- The last step is to prepare an individual serving of vigorón for each person at the table: use medium-sized plates. Place a small portion of cabbage (about ½ cup) on the plate, and top with about 4 tablespoons of the diced-tomato mixture, about 3 or so pieces of cooked pork, and 3 pieces of yuca; place a couple of lime quarters on the side of the plate (squeeze the lime on top of the pork, both to add taste and to "cut" the grease).

Note: In Nicaragua and some parts of Costa Rica, vigorón is traditionally served on banana leaves. Besides making a great presentation, the leaves reputedly impart a subtle additional flavor to the dish.

Breakfast in Costa Rica

The traditional Tico breakfast was a hearty meal that included gallo pinto with a dab of sour cream (usually served with tortillas), eggs, cooked plantains, and, sometimes, another dish or two—chorreadas perhaps! And there was always fresh fruit and either coffee or agua dulce.

In some places in Costa Rica, especially in rural areas, this very filling breakfast—or a variant—is still eaten. In much of the country, however, as the rhythm of life has become faster, the traditional breakfast has given way to breakfasts that are quicker to prepare (and easier on the waistline). Today, a simple breakfast might consist of a single egg served with bread, or bread with either cheese, sour cream, or jam. And many people go with just cereal and milk. (The traditional breakfast was appropriate when most Costa Ricans were farmers and their work required lots of physical labor. Nowadays, when the majority of people work in offices and stores, most people prefer to start the day with a lighter meal.)

Coffee and fruits such as banana, papaya, mango, canteloupe, and watermelon are still breakfast staples. Agua dulce, however, has pretty much been replaced by orange juice in most parts of the country.

Desserts

and Treats for Coffee Hour

Ayote Flan / Flan de ayote

(6 - 8 servings)

Flan de ayote is a traditional Costa Rican dessert whose basic ingredients are ayote, egg yolks, milk, and sugar. To this can be added coffee, orange, vanilla extract, and other flavors.

Ingredients:

- 2 lbs. of ripe ayote.
- 4 eggs.
- 5 tablespoons of flour.
- 2 cups sugar.
- 1 can of evaporated milk (12 oz.).
- 2 tablespoons of butter, melted.
- vanilla extract (to taste).

Preparation:

- Preheat the oven to medium.
- Slice up the ayote into medium-sized pieces (note: the exact size of the pieces doesn't matter); place the ayote in a pot and cover with water. Bring to a boil and then

simmer until the ayote is soft enough to purée. (If you're short on time, you can microwave it instead.)

- Drain the ayote and let it cool off for a couple of minutes. Remove the skin and discard, but set aside the pulp.
- In a blender, purée the following: half of the ayote pulp, 2 eggs, 2 ½ tablespoons of flour, 1 cup of sugar, and half of the evaporated milk. Store the resulting mixture, then purée the remaining pulp, eggs, flour, sugar, and milk. (This is done in 2 steps because most blenders can't handle all the ingredients at one go.)
- Put both batches into a large bowl. Add the melted butter and the vanilla extract and stir.
- Place the mixture in a greased, ovenproof dish and set that inside of a larger roasting pan. Carefully fill the space between the dish and the roasting pan with ½ inch of hot water. Bake until golden brown.
- Refrigerate the flan and serve cold.

Baked Tamal / Tamal asado
(12 - 15 servings)

This dessert tamal is quite different in taste from the pork- and bean-filled tamales you've eaten in Mexican restaurants. Baked tamal is also easier to prepare than the standard tamal—and you don't need to wrap it in banana leaves prior to cooking. (See cultural note about tamales on pp. 124-125.)

Ingredients:

- 1 lb. of corn flour.
- 1 cup buttermilk.

- 2 cups sugar.
- ¼ teaspoon of salt.
- 1 cup of mild cheese, grated.
- 1 cup sour cream.
- 2 sticks of butter, melted.
- ¼ teaspoon of vanilla.
- ¼ teaspoon of ground cinnamon.

Preparation:

- Preheat the oven to medium.
- In a large bowl, mix the corn flour with the buttermilk, sugar, salt, cheese, and sour cream.
- While continuing to stir, add in the butter, vanilla, and cinnamon.
- Place the batter in a pot and heat over medium-high for a couple of minutes. Keep stirring to prevent the ingredients from sticking.
- Pour the mixture into a well-greased ovenproof baking dish and bake until a golden color—about 30 minutes or until a knife inserted in the center comes out clean.

Banana Cake /
Queque de banano
(makes an 8-inch-diameter round cake)

Though not native to the Americas, the banana tree now thrives here, especially in Central and South America. Indeed, today it is one of the most popular fruits in Costa Rica—and one of the country's biggest exports.

Ingredients:

- 2 cups flour.
- 4 tablespoons of baking powder.
- 1 tablespoon of ground cloves.
- 1 tablespoon of ground nutmeg.
- 9 ripe bananas.
- 1 stick of butter.
- 1 ½ cups sugar.
- 2 eggs.
- 1 cup milk.
- 1 teaspoon of vanilla extract.

Preparation:

- Preheat the oven to medium.
- Combine the flour and baking powder and sift; to the sifted powder, add in the cloves and nutmeg. Set aside.
- In another bowl, mash the bananas. Mix in the butter, sugar, eggs, milk, and vanilla extract. Continue to stir and gradually fold in the flour mixture.
- Pour the batter into a greased, round cake pan.
- Bake for approximately one hour, until firm enough so that a knife inserted in the center comes out clean.

Buñuelos

(18 - 20 pastries)

Buñuelos—petite, delicious, "honey"-covered pastries—are a traditional favorite of people in rural areas of Costa Rica.

Ingredients:

- 20 oz. (1 block) of tapa de dulce.
- 2 cups of corn flour.
- ½ cup mild cheese, grated.
- ½ cup raw yuca, grated.
- 2 sticks of butter, melted.
- vegetable oil.

Preparation:

- Place the tapa de dulce and a dash of water in a saucepan; cook over medium heat until the tapa de dulce melts and reaches the consistency of honey. Set aside.
- In a deep bowl, mix together the corn flour, cheese, yuca, and melted butter; continue to mix until the ingredients take on a doughy consistency.
- With this dough, make 1-inch balls; fry them in a little oil until they turn a golden color.
- Remove the buñuelo balls; put them on paper towels to drain; then place on a plate and drizzle on the tapa de dulce.
- Serve hot.

Cheese Tortillas /
Tortillas de queso
(12 - 14 tortillas)

Cheese tortillas are larger and thicker than regular corn tortillas. While corn tortillas are served to accompany a main dish, cheese tortillas are a tasty treat all by themselves, either at a mid-morniing coffee break or in the afternoon.

- 2 cups corn flour.
- ¼ cup water.
- 2 cups of a mild white cheese, grated.
- salt (to taste).
- sour cream.

Preparation:

- Put the corn flour in a deep bowl. Knead while adding water little by little until you get an even-textured dough that has lost its stickiness.
- Add in the cheese and knead again.
- To make each tortilla, shape 3 tablespoons of the dough into a ball. Place it on cling wrap or waxed paper, and then lay another sheet over the dough. Flatten the ball with a pan or plate and finish flattening it with your fingers so that it is as even as possible. You can also use a tortilla press.
- Fry the tortillas on both sides in a pan with a little vegetable oil, or cook them without any oil in a nonstick pan.
- Top with sour cream (or grated cheese) and serve hot.

Chiverre Empanadas /
Empanadas de chiverre
(10 - 12 empanadas)

Chiverre is a delicious squash that is quite similar to pumpkin. It comes into season during the same time of year as Easter, and in Costa Rica these dessert empanadas—along with chiverre jelly—are as closely linked with Easter week celebrations as pumpkin pie is linked with Thanksgiving. Chiverre empanadas are smaller than those made from corn flour or plantain, but they are every bit as tasty. (Nowadays, many people prefer to buy pre-prepared chiverre filling in the supermarket. If you are unable to locate either the fruit or the prepared filling, you can use pineapple jelly—or any other jelly or fruit preserve—as a substitute.)

Ingredients for the dough:

- 3 cups flour.
- ¾ cup of butter (1 ½ sticks).
- 3 tablespoons of sugar.
- 1 carton of whipping cream (9 oz.).

Ingredients for the filling:

- 1 chiverre.
- 20 oz. (1 block) of tapa de dulce.
- ground cloves (to taste).
- ground cinammon (to taste).
- 2 fig leaves.

Preparing the dough:

- Put the flour in a bowl. Add in the butter and sugar and mix with a fork until the mixture takes on the appearance of tiny breadcrumbs.
- Add the whipping cream little by little and knead until the dough comes away from the sides of the bowl and forms a ball.

Preparing the filling:

- Chiverres have a very hard rind. To open the squash, hit it repeatedly with a hammer until the rind cracks; insert a thick-bladed knife into the split and pry it open. (If you have a large oven, you can try another method: place the chiverre in the oven on medium heat until the rind burns or peels off; let it cool, and then you can hammer open the squash more easily—and you'll need to cook it for less time later on.)
- Once the chiverre has been opened, remove the pulp and set it aside—and discard the seeds.
- Cook the pulp in boiling water until soft.
- Take the pot off the stove; remove any fibrous or stringy parts from the chiverre; strain off the water.
- To a large pot, add the pulp, tapa de dulce, cloves, cinnamon, and fig leaves; cook over medium heat until the ingredients reach the consistency of honey.

Making the empanadas:

- Preheat oven to medium.
- Sprinkle flour over a large surface; knead the ball of dough briefly, then flatten it with a rolling pin.
- Use a round cookie cutter (not the fluted kind) or the rim of a glass to cut out circles of dough. Add about a

teaspoon of the chiverre mixture to each circle, fold it in half, and press along the edge with a fork to seal it—and to make sure the filling does not fall out.
- Grease a shallow, ovenproof glass dish (or cookie sheet); lay out the empanadas and bake until they turn a golden color.
- Remove from oven and let cool before serving.

Chorreadas
(8 - 10 chorreadas)

Chorreadas (from the verb *chorrear*—to pour) are thin corn pancakes that are served at breakfast or with afternoon coffee. Today, the fast pace of life in urban Costa Rica doesn't allow most people the luxury of a leisurely breakfast—quick breakfasts of toast or cereal are increasingly the norm. But chorreadas are still on the menu in restaurants that serve traditional food. And they are still very popular throughout the countryside, particularly during corn harvest. (This dish is also served at some restaurants that cater to tourists; at these restauarants, chorreadas are often served with honey or syrup—as though they were pancakes.)

Ingredients:

- 2 ½ cups corn kernels.
- ½ cup flour.
- 2 eggs (yolks and whites).
- ½ cup milk.
- ⅛ teaspoon of salt.

- ½ cup sugar.
- ½ tablespoon of vanilla extract.
- vegetable oil.
- sour cream (or mild cheese, grated).

Preparation:

- In a food processor or blender, mix all ingredients (except vegetable oil and sour cream) until smooth.
- Heat a small amount of vegetable oil in a skillet over medium heat.
- For each chorreada pour six tablespoons of batter into the pan and spread them to form a large, thin pancake. Fry each side about 3 minutes, or until golden.
- Top with sour cream and/or grated cheese. Serve hot.

Coconut Flan / Flan de coco
(10 - 12 servings)

Coconut flan is the most commonly served flan in Costa Rica; it appears on the dessert menus of most restaurants in the country. If you're curious about why this is such a popular dish, we suggest you go ahead and make the recipe!

Ingredients for the flan:

- 5 eggs.
- 1 ¾ cups condensed milk.
- 1 ¾ cups milk (or evaporated milk).

- 5 tablespoons of sugar.
- 2 cups grated coconut (fresh or dried).
- 1 tablespoon of vanilla.

Ingredients for the caramel:

- 1 cup sugar.
- ¼ cup water.
- ¼ teaspoon of butter.

Preparation:

- Preheat the oven to medium.
- Place all the flan ingredients into a blender and mix thoroughly. Set aside.
- To prepare the caramel, heat the sugar and the water in a small pot until the sugar dissolves and thickens. Once it reaches a honey-like consistency, add the butter and remove the pot from the stove. Stir well.
- Pour the caramel into a baking dish, making sure to cover the bottom of the dish completely. Immediately add in the flan mixture.
- Place the baking dish inside of a larger roasting pan. Carefully fill the space between the dish and the roasting pan with a ½ inch of hot water.

- Bake until a knife inserted into the center of the flan comes out clean.

Note: When the flan is ready to serve, you can pour some of the caramel sauce that remains in the baking pan over the top of the flan. To vary this recipe, you can substitute the following fruits for the coconut: chopped figs, pineapple, or drained canned fruits.

Corn Flour Empanadas /
Empanadas de masa
(10 - 12 empanadas)

An empanada is a type of non-dessert pastry filled with meat, cheese, or any number of other ingredients. (The Spanish verb *empanar* means "to wrap something in dough.") Although the empanada is more closely identified with Argentina or Chile, corn-flour empanadas are one of the favorite dishes in Costa Rica. Here, most coffee shops and sodas (simple restaurants with low-cost fare) serve empanadas, and they are eaten at any time of the day, often with coffee or fruit-juice drinks.

Ingredients:

- 2 cups corn flour.
- ½ cup of water.
- salt (to taste).
- 1 ½ cups mild, white cheese, grated (or refried beans; see recipe on p. 38).
- vegetable oil.

Preparation:

- Put the corn flour, water, and salt in a bowl and mix to form dough.
- Shape the dough into balls slightly smaller than your fist and place each on a piece of cling wrap or waxed paper. Flatten the balls of dough into round, flat tortilla-like shapes.
- Scoop a tablespoon of cheese or refried beans and place on the center of the circle-shaped dough. Next, fold over the circle to form a half-moon shape.
- Pinch along the entire edge of the empanada to seal it—and to prevent the filling from spilling out.
- Repeat the process until you've finished the entire batch of empanadas.
- Heat about 1 inch of vegetable oil in a heavy skillet. When the oil is hot, fry the empanadas in batches, turning them with a slotted spoon, until they are a golden color on both sides (this usually takes about 4 minutes).
- Drain the empanadas on paper towels and serve immediately.

Note: You can use other fillings such as ground beef, shredded chicken, and picadillo.

Corn Pudding /
Pudín de elote
(4 - 6 servings)

This filling dessert has a flavor somewhat similar to cornbread, but it is much moister and sweeter, and has a finer consistency. It is absolutely delicious—and surprisingly easy to make!

Ingredients:

- 1 can condensed milk (14 oz.).
- 1 can sweet corn (15 oz.).
- 4 eggs.

Preparation:

- Preheat the oven to medium.
- Blend all the ingredients in a food processor or blender.
- Grease a medium-sized ovenproof glass dish. Pour the mixture into the dish and bake for about 30 minutes, or until firm enough so that a knife inserted in the center comes out clean.
- Allow to cool and serve at room temperature.

Note: Although the corn kernels will be minced in the food processor, small bits will remain in the final dish. If you prefer a smoother pudding, put the corn and the eggs in the food processor first and blend them. Strain the mixture, add the condensed milk, and blend again.

Homemade bread / Pan casero

(2 loaves)

Ticos like to eat bread along with breakfast—and even with their afternoon coffee. Although most families now buy bread instead of making it, for many people—especially those in rural areas—homemade bread is still a must. This recipe produces a bread that is neither sweet nor salty, so it goes well with sour cream, butter, cheese, and even jam.

Ingredients:

- ½ teaspoon of yeast.
- ¾ cup of warm water.
- ¾ cup of sugar.
- 6 tablespoons of butter.
- ⅛ cup of milk.
- 4 ¾ cups flour.

Preparation:

- In a bowl, dissolve the yeast in warm water. Cover the bowl and set aside for 10 minutes.
- Add the sugar, butter, and milk to the yeast. Finally, add the flour, stirring as you add.
- Knead all the ingredients to form a smooth dough. Cover again and set aside for two hours to give time for the dough to rise.
- Divide the dough in half, make two rounded loaves, and set aside for another hour.
- Preheat the oven to medium.
- Bake dough in greased loaf pans until golden brown.

Mazamorra

(10 - 12 servings)

Mazamorra is a traditional corn dessert with a puddinglike texture. Today you can order this delicious dish at fairs and in restaurants where home-style cooking is served. In San José at the beginning of the 20th century, this dessert was such a staple at neighborhood dances that people grew accostmed to referring to these events as mazamorras.[1] Thus it was common to hear "Come on, let's go to the mazamorra!"

Ingredients:

- 24 ears of uncooked corn.
- 20 oz. (1 block) of tapa de dulce.
- 2 pieces of ginger (each approximately ¾ inch x ¾ inch).
- ¼ teaspoon of salt.
- 4 cups milk.

Preparation:

- Husk the corn and cut the kernels from the cob. Add the kernels and a dash of water to a blender and purée.
- Leave the corn out, unrefrigerated, until the following day; the kernels should have acquired a slightly sour taste. Strain the mixture through a fine sieve, discarding the solids that remain in the sieve. Place the corn liquid in a pot and set aside for an hour or so. The corn liquid will settle to the bottom of the pot and the water will separate and rise to form a layer on the surface. Decant off the water and set aside the now nearly pure corn liquid.

1. *Entre el comal y la olla. Marjorie Ross.*

- Place a dash of water in a pan and melt the tapa de dulce over medium heat.
- Place the corn liquid in a pot over medium heat; add in the melted tapa de dulce and the ginger and salt. Stir constantly with a wooden spoon. When the mixture begins to thicken (and starts bubbling rapidly), take the pot off the stove and remove the pieces of ginger.
- Gradually add 4 cups of milk to the mixture and stir until it has a thick consistency. Serve immediately in small dessert bowls.

Milk Cajetas /
Cajetas de leche
(15 - 20 individual cajetas)

Cajeta is a fudge-like candy that in yesteryear was served in little boxes (in Spanish, *cajetas*). Varieties range from chocolate to coconut—and even include fruit flavors like papaya—although cajetas are made from milk. In the province of Guanacaste, cajetas were formerly an essential dish at weddings, where nosy people were often heard to ask an unwed couple: "so, when are we going to eat cajeta?"[1]

Ingredients:

- 2 cups condensed milk.
- 1 cup powdered milk.
- 1 ½ tablespoons of butter.

1. *Cocina Tradicional Costarricense*. Ministerio de Cultura Juventud y Deportes.

Preparation:

- Cream all the ingredients together in a bowl until you have a smooth paste. No cooking is required.
- Take the paste and shape it into small balls; place each ball in a small version of the traditional cupcake papers.
- Either refrigerate the cajetas to serve cold later or eat them immediately.

Note: You can decorate an individual cajeta by topping with a raisin, a dried nut or two, or candied fruit.

Plantain Empanadas /
Empanadas de plátano
(8 - 10 empanadas)

In Costa Rica—and elsewhere—empanadas are of many kinds; the pastry dough can be made from cornmeal, flour, or, as here, even plantain; the stuffing consists of a wide range of ingredients—ranging from salty to sweet;

and, you fry some empanadas but bake others. This recipe calls for dough made from plantains (sweetened with sugar) and a stuffing of either cheese or refried beans—the combination of sweet and salty is delicious.

Ingredients:

- 4 ripe plantains.
- 2 teaspoons of sugar.
- 1 cup of mild white cheese, grated (or refried beans; see recipe on p. 38).
- vegetable oil.

Preparation:

- Peel the plantains and boil them in water until they are soft.
- Drain the plantains and mash them with a large fork or potato masher. Add the sugar and mix well.
- Use this mixture to form a ball just slightly smaller than your fist and place the ball on a piece of cling wrap or waxed paper. Flatten the ball out into a circle, as if it were a tortilla.
- Scoop a tablespoon of cheese or refried beans onto the middle of the circle. Then fold the circle in half (use the cling wrap or waxed paper to help you). This should result in a half-moon shape.
- Press the edges together to seal the empanada (and to prevent the filling from spilling out).
- Repeat the process and continue making empanadas until you have used up all the ingredients.
- Heat about 1 inch of vegetable oil in a heavy skillet. When the oil is hot, fry the empanadas in batches, turning them with a slotted spoon until they are golden on both sides (takes about 4 minutes).
- Drain the empanadas on paper towels and serve immediately.

Pound Cake /
Queque seco

(this recipe makes a 9" by 5" cake)

In Costa Rica, pound cake is known as queque seco—literally, "dry cake." It is prepared in a variety of ways and is eaten with afternoon coffee or as a dessert. For birthday celebrations, Costa Ricans usually shun pound cake, preferring instead more elaborate recipes that call for fillings and icings.

Ingredients:

- 2 cups flour.
- 2 teaspoons of baking powder.
- 2 sticks of butter.
- 1 cup sugar.
- 1 teaspoon of vanilla extract.
- 6 eggs.
- 1 cup milk.
- 1 cup orange juice.
- raisins to taste (optional).

Preparation:

- Preheat the oven to medium.
- Combine flour and baking powder and sift. Set aside.
- With a fork mix together the butter, sugar, and vanilla extract until the ingredients reach a creamy texture. Beat in the eggs one at a time. While continuing to stir, add in a small portion of the powdered mixture, then some of the milk, and finally some of the orange juice. Repeat until you have added in all the ingredients. Mix thoroughly.
- Add the raisins, if using. Mix well with a fork or large spoon.
- Pour the batter into a greased cake pan and bake for about 45 minutes, or until a knife inserted in the center comes out clean.

Prestiños
(6 - 8 prestiños)

The prestiño is a crunchy fritter that is eaten with a specially prepared syrup. Although this dish is well known throughout the country, it's especially popular in the province of Puntarenas.

Ingredients:

- 1 ¼ cups flour.
- 1 teaspoon of sugar.
- ½ teaspoon of salt.
- 1 egg yolk.

- 2 ¼ cups of water.
- vegetable oil.
- 20 oz. (1 block) of tapa de dulce.

Preparation:

- Mix together the flour, sugar, and salt.
- In another bowl, combine the egg yolk and ¼ cup of water, then stir this into the bowl containing the flour, sugar, and salt. Mix thoroughly to create a dough.
- Roll out the dough very thinly on a floured board.
- Using a medium-sized plate as a pattern, cut circles out of the dough.
- Fry each circle in vegetable oil until it is golden brown and swells up on both sides. Remove, place on paper towels.
- To make the syrup: Over medium heat, bring to a boil the remaining 2 cups of water and the tapa de dulce. Continue to boil until it thickens into a syrup.
- Drizzle syrup over each prestiño and serve at room temperature.

Rice Pudding /
Arroz con leche
(8 servings)

This traditional dessert is a Costa Rican favorite.

Ingredients:

- 2 cups of rice.
- grated lime rind (from half a lime).
- 1 tablespoon of butter.
- 3 cups of water.
- 1 can condensed milk (14 oz.).
- 1 can evaporated milk (12 oz.).
- ½ cup of raisins or one diced apple (first cook the apple in a microwave to soften it). Some people add raisins and apple.
- rum to taste (or 1 tablespoon of vanilla extract).
- ½ teaspoon of ground cinammon.

Preparation:

- Add the rice, lime rind, and butter to cold water. Bring the water to a boil, then reduce heat to low, cover pot, and continue cooking until rice is very soft—much softer than if you were preparing rice as a side dish. (If cooking with whole grain rice, you will probably need to use a little more water.)
- When the rice is thoroughly cooked, add in both the condensed milk and the evaporated milk. Simmer over medium-low heat, stirring constantly so that the rice doesn't stick; continue cooking until the mixture begins to thicken.

- Add the raisins and/or apple and let the pudding thicken a little more.
- Turn the heat to low, add the rum or vanilla extract, stir well, and sprinkle with cinnamon. This dish can be served hot or cold.

Note: If you prefer, you can use regular milk (sweetened with sugar) to replace both the evaporated and the condensed milk.

Tres Leches
(8 - 10 servings)

Tres leches is a delicious, sweet, spongy cake that is soaked in a mixture of three kinds of milk—regular, evaporated, and condensed—hence the name. Although this dessert is perhaps not as popular in rural areas as, say, buñuelos or prestiños, it has gradually become the most popular dessert in Costa Rica.

Ingredients for the cake:

- 6 eggs (whites and yolks separated).
- 1 cup flour.
- 1 teaspoon of baking powder.
- 1 cup sugar.

Ingredients for the creamy topping:

- 1 can condensed milk (14 oz.).
- 1 can evaporated milk (12 oz.).
- 1 cup milk.
- 1 cup whipping cream.
- rum to taste (optional).

Ingredients for the meringue:

- whites of 3 eggs.
- 5 tablespoons of sugar.
- 1 teaspoon of vanilla.

Preparation:

- Preheat the oven to medium.
- Beat the 6 egg whites until stiff peaks form. Place in a large bowl.
- Combine the flour and baking powder and sift into a second bowl.
- To the egg whites, gradually add in the dry ingredients, egg yolks, and sugar. Mix well.
- Pour the mixture into a greased ovenproof pan and bake for 30 to 40 minutes, or until a knife inserted in the center comes out clean.
- While the cake is baking, blend together the three kinds of milk and the whipping cream. You can also add a little rum, if you like.
- When the cake is ready, remove it from the oven and prick the top several times with a fork. Pour the creamy topping over the hot cake, soaking it well. Allow the cake to cool completely.
- Make the meringue by beating 3 egg whites until stiff peaks form. Add in the sugar and vanilla.
- When the cake has cooled off, spread the meringue over the top. Refrigerate well before serving.

Coffee and Costa Rican Culture

Coffee—its production and consumption—is a vital aspect of life in Costa Rica. The great majority of Ticos drink coffee not only with meals but also during mid-morning and mid-afternoon coffee breaks. In fact, the coffee break is such a customary feature of daily life that many businesses give their employees both a lunch break and two 15-minute coffee breaks.

The traditional way to make coffee is to put a little ground coffee into a sock-shaped cloth bag that is suspended above a pitcher or other receptacle. Boiling water is slowly poured over the grounds as they are gently stirred. The freshly strained coffee is poured from the pitcher into cups and served with sugar and milk. In recent years, however, the traditional method of preparing coffee has been almost completely replaced by the use of modern coffeemakers. Nonetheless, the Tico appetite for coffee remains unabated.

How, you may ask, did coffee become such an important aspect of national culture? Coffee was first imported from the Antilles in the first decades of the 19th Century. Thereafter, the government so successfully promoted its commercial cultivation that it came to represent 80 to 90 percent of the country's total exports during the period between 1850 and 1890. And, unlike in other Central American countries, ownership of coffee farms was more equitably distributed, so that the resulting wealth was also more widely distributed.

Coffee, then, allowed tiny Costa Rica to participate in the international market for goods—and to reap all the benefits that this fact implied. And on a national level, coffee profits financed Costa Rica's development as well as the emergence of a powerful group of leading coffee producers whose influence on the country's politics and culture would be lasting.

Today, the production of *grano de oro* (literally, the "golden bean") is no longer the country's primary source of national revenue, but Costa Rican coffee—considered some of the finest in the world—is still a very important part of the economy and culture.

Drinks

Agua Dulce

Agua dulce (literally "sweet water") is a hot drink made from tapa de dulce—also known as panela or piloncillo in other parts of Latin America—a block, or ingot, of unrefined sugarcane. Until fairly recently, agua dulce (and coffee) were the two most typical breakfast beverages. Today, however, most families drink orange juice and/ or coffee in the morning, although tapa de dulce is still readily available in most Costa Rican supermarkets. You can substitute unrefined brown sugar for tapa de dulce if you can't find the latter in your local supermarket.

Ingredients:

- 20 oz. (1 block) of tapa de dulce.
- water.

Preparation:

- Pour three cups of water into a pot and boil the tapa de dulce for approximately 15 minutes; stir occasionally and continue to cook until it melts into a thick syrup.

- To another pot, add a cup of water for every serving of agua dulce you want to make; boil. Add one tablespoon of the syrup for each cup of water and stir until dissolved.
- Serve hot. If you prefer a sweeter drink, add a little more of the syrup. Some people also like to add in a little milk.

Note: To store leftover syrup, place it in a covered container and refrigerate.

Corn Chicha /
Chicha de maíz
(16 servings)

Chichas are a class of fermented alcoholic beverages that date back to Pre-Columbian times—and are still popular today in Peru and several other countries in Latin America! Costa Rican cuisine includes several kinds of chicha, though the most common version is made from corn.

Ingredients:

- 2 lbs. of ground corn.
- 2 ½ gallons of water.
- 30 oz. (1 ½ blocks) of tapa de dulce.
- ¼ cup of ground ginger.

Preparation:

- Put the corn in a large pot and add ½ gallon of water.

- Boil over high heat for about 25 minutes. Then drain the corn and place it in a large wooden bowl.
- Place the tapa de dulce and a little water in a small saucepan; over medium heat, melt the tapa de dulce until it has the consistency of honey.
- To the corn, add 2 gallons cold water, the melted tapa de dulce, and the ginger.
- Cover the wooden bowl with a cloth and store it at room temperature for 5 days. Drain the mixture through a fine strainer, separating the solids from the liquid (chica).
- Serve cold or at room temperature.

Fresh Fruit Drink /
Fresco de frutas

You will seldom enter a Costa Rican home without being offered a delicious fresco, which is the generic word to describe any drink made from the juice of fresh fruits; in some cases water or milk is added. The fresco is served cold, at lunch or dinner—or as a refreshing beverage between meals (thus the name *fresco*, from *refrescarse*—to refresh).

Ingredients:

- fruit of choice (pineapple, guava, cas, soursop fruit, melon, watermelon, etc.)
- water.
- sugar.

Preparation:

- Peel and liquefy the fruit in a blender, and, if necessary, strain the juice. If you select a citrus fruit such as lime, you of course only need to squeeze the fruit to obtain juice.
- Add water and sugar to taste.
- Serve with ice.

Note: You can combine two or more fruits. Also, if you make a papaya or soursop fruit (guanábana) fresco, you can use milk instead of water.

Fruit Drink with Syrup /
Fresco de frutas con sirope
(6 servings)

This is a delicious variant on the fresco theme.

Ingredients:

- 6 cups of water.
- ½ cup Kola Rojo syrup (a local version of Grenadine syrup).
- 2 cups mixed fruits (banana, papaya, and pineapple, preferably fresh, finely chopped).

Preparation:

- Combine the water and syrup; add the chopped fruit. Stir.
- Serve cold.

Guaro Sour
(1 cocktail)

This very popular Tico cocktail tastes quite similar to a whisky sour. The guaro sour has only gained popularity

in modern times, though its key ingredient, guaro, has been popular from way back. Guaro—essentially sugarcane spirts—has a somewhat neutral flavor. This makes it suitable for drinking straight or for mixing with cocktails.

Ingredients:

- 1 oz. guaro.
- 1 1/3 cups of orange juice.
- 1 or 2 oz. of soda water mixed with equal parts sugar (you may adjust the proportions depending on how sweet you like it).
- 1 oz. of lime juice.

Preparation:

- Mix all the ingredients together and serve over ice.

Horchata

(8 - 10 servings)

This wonderfully unique and delicious beverage hails from Guanacaste, where it was once the obligatory drink at birthday celebrations.[2] Preparing horchata is a somewhat complex process, so today many Ticos prefer to make this drink from a powdered mix available in supermarkets.

Ingredients:

- 1 cup rice.
- 1 cup of unsalted peanuts, shelled.
- 1 tablespoon of ground cinnamon.
- 10 cups milk.
- 1 tablespoon of vanilla.
- sugar (to taste).
- 2 tablespoons of powdered cocoa.

Preparation:

- Soak the rice in water sufficient to just cover it and set aside for at least two hours (some people prefer to soak the rice overnight); drain and discard the water.
- In a blender, purée the rice, peanuts, and cinnamon with five cups of milk, then strain. Add the remaining milk, the vanilla, sugar, and cocoa and mix thoroughly.
- Serve very cold.

2. *Entre el comal y la olla*. Marjorie Ross.

Resbaladera

(8 - 10 servings)

Resbaladera, a drink made from rice, milk, and (sometimes) barley, is especially popular in the Costa Rican provinces of Guanacaste and Puntarenas.

Ingredients:

- 2 cups water.
- 1 cup rice.
- ¼ teaspoon of ground cloves.
- 1 teaspoon of ground cinnamon.
- ½ teaspoon of ground nutmeg.
- 8 cups milk.
- 2 tablespoons of vanilla extract.
- sugar (to taste).
- crushed ice (to taste).

Preparation:

- Soak the rice and ground cloves in 2 cups of water for one hour. Pour the mixture into a blender and purée until smooth.
- Pour the contents into a pot; add in the cinnamon and nutmeg and cook over medium heat for 15 minutes, stirring constantly.
- Remove from heat and allow to cool. In a blender, combine the rice mixture with the milk, vanilla extract, and sugar; purée.
- Strain and serve over crushed ice.

Christmas
dishes

Bean Tamal /
Tamal de frijol

Bean tamales are very popular during Holy Week—the week before Easter—when the Catholic Church, to which most Costa Ricans belong, forbids the eating of meat. At any time of the year, though, they make a delicious meal.

Ingredients:

- ½ recipe for tamale dough (see recipe on p. 120; follow that recipe but do not add the bacon or pork lard).
- A double recipe of refried beans (see recipe on p. 38).

Wrapping the tamales:

- 1 ball of kitchen twine or thin strips of corn husk (to tie the tamales).
- 100 tender banana leaves (it is important to clean them well on both sides).

Making the tamales:

- Follow the instructions for the pork tamales (p. 120), but—since bean tamales are smaller than pork tamales—use only 1 heaping tablespoon of dough for each. Place the dough on top of a banana leaf and put a teaspoon of beans onto the dough.
- Fold, tie, and cook as indicated in the recipe for pork tamales, but reduce cooking time to 1 ½ hours.

Christmas Cake /
Queque de Navidad

(makes two 4" x 8 ½" loaves, or several smaller cakes)

This rum-soaked, dense cake is chock-full of nuts, raisins (or prunes), and candied fruit. During the holiday season, many people make small cakes to give as gifts to family and friends, and these gifts are much appreciated, as it takes quite a bit of time to prepare Christmas cakes. Because of that, some people prefer to buy these cakes at the grocery store or bakery, where they are generally available during the Christmas season.

Ingredients for the cake:

- ½ lb. candied fruit.
- ½ lb. raisins or prunes.
- rum (to taste).
- 10 eggs.
- 1 lb. butter.
- 1 cup brown sugar.
- 4 cups flour.
- 6 teaspoons of baking powder.
- 1 teaspoon of ground cinnamon.
- 1 teaspoon of ground cloves.

- ½ teaspoon of ground nutmeg.
- 1 can condensed milk (14 oz.).
- ½ lb. shelled   pecans, almonds, walnuts, macadamia nuts, or peanuts.

Ingredients for the syrup:

- ½ cup brown sugar.
- 1 ½ cups water.
- rum (to taste).

Preparation:

- A week prior to preparing the cake, soak the candied fruits and raisins in rum and set aside.
- Preheat the oven to medium.
- Beat the eggs and set aside.
- In a separate, large bowl, cream the butter and sugar; set aside.
- Sift together the flour, baking powder, and spices.
- To the sugar and butter mixture, first add the dry ingredients, then, while continuing to beat, gradually add in the eggs; then add in the condensed milk.
- Finally, use a wooden spoon to fold in the candied fruits and raisins and any rum that hasn't been absorbed. Finally, fold in the nuts. Mix well.
- Pour the batter into greased and floured loaf pans and bake for about one hour.
- To make the syrup: In a pan over medium heat, combine the brown sugar with the water, and add rum to taste. Stir until smooth, making sure it doesn't come to a boil.
- Once the cake is done, allow it to cool and pour the brown sugar syrup over it.

Note: The cake can be cut into smaller pieces and wrapped in aluminum foil to preserve freshness. You can also freeze the cake.

Eggnog / Rompope
(4 - 6 servings)

This version of eggnog is said to have been created in the 17th century by the Poor Clare Sisters of Spain.[3] They brought the recipe to Mexico whence it spread to many other parts of the American continent. In Costa Rican homes, rompope is prepared for parties during the Christmas season, although it can be purchased year-round at most grocery stores.

Ingredients:

- 4 cups milk.
- 1 ½ tablespoons of corn starch.
- 3 egg yolks, beaten.

3. Marjorie Ross.

- 1 cup of sugar.
- ½ teaspoon of vanilla extract.
- ¼ teaspoon of ground nutmeg.
- 1 cup of rum.
- 2 sticks of cinnamon, ground.

Preparation:

- Dissolve the corn starch in a little of the milk.
- Mix the rest of the milk into the dissolved corn starch, and add in the egg yolks, sugar, vanilla extract, and nutmeg.
- Heat the mixture in a saucepan over medium heat, stirring constantly.
- As soon as the liquid comes to a boil, remove it from the heat; allow to cool then refrigerate.
- Once cold, blend with the rum, sprinkle with cinnamon, and serve.

Pork Tamal /
Tamal de cerdo
(ingredients for 100 tamales, or 50 piñas)

In Costa Rica, pork tamales are arguably the most representative recipe of the Christmas season, when it is customary to invite friends and family members over for a coffee and a tamal, and to present as a gift the piña (two individually wrapped tamales tied together). Tamales are also the main course of the traditional Christmas dinner.

Ingredients for the dough:

- 20 lbs. medium potatoes.
- 11 lbs. dried corn, prepared and ground for tamales (or corn flour).
- 3 lbs. thick-cut bacon.
- Spices:
  - 2 sprigs of thyme.
  - 5 sprigs of oregano.
  - 5 bay leaves.
  - 2 heads of garlic, cloves separated and peeled.
  - paprika (to taste).
  - curry powder (to taste).
  - Complete Seasoning.
- 1 ½ cups water.
- 1 lb. pork lard (or vegetable shortening).
- 1 ½ lbs. of well roasted (or fried) pork rib meat, minced.
- 1 medium jar of mustard.
- 1 ½ tablespoons of salt.
- 5 tablespoons of Worcester sauce.

Ingredients for the filling:

- 4 ½ lbs. of pork loin (or boneless pork chops), marinated in olive oil and rosemary.
- 2 lbs. of rice (with achiote).

- 3 red bell peppers, cut into strips.
- 100 pitted prunes (optional).
- 100 pitted green olives (approx. 2 small jars).
- fresh or frozen peas: an amount equivalent to 2 medium cans.
- 300 chickpeas: an amount equivalent to 2 medium cans.
- 3 large carrots, sliced.

Wrapping the tamales:

- 1 ball of kitchen twine (or thin strips of corn husk) to tie the tamales.
- 200 tender banana leaves, cleaned on both sides and cut into 2 sizes:
  - 100 leaves cut into squares of 10" x 10".
  - 100 leaves cut into squares of 16" x 16".

Special utensils:

- Large pot and large aluminum serving spoon or ladle.

Preparing the dough:

- Scrub the potatoes thoroughly and boil without peeling. Cook until tender, then peel the potatoes (while still hot) and mash.
- Mix the mashed potatoes with the ground corn until the mixture reaches a consistency between the smooth texture of a potato purée and the granular consistency of cornmeal dough. Set aside.
- In a large pan, fry the bacon along with all the spices, and then add the water; set aside.
- In a separate pot, combine the lard and the pork rib meat, and bring to a simmer. Add in the cooked bacon and spices. Continue cooking for a short while.

- Pour the ingredients into a blender or food processor, and blend thoroughly. Strain while the ingredients are still hot.
- Discard the solids left in the strainer; to the remaining liquid, add the mustard, salt, and Worcester sauce. Combine this mixture with the potato and ground corn purée and mix well. Taste for seasoning and set aside to allow the dough to rise a bit before assembling the tamales.

Preparing the filling:

- Cut the marinated pork loin into 2-inch squares. Set aside.
- Brown the rice and achiote in a skillet with a little vegetable oil. Set aside.
- Take the remaining ingredients for the filling and place each in separate dishes, so that these are readily at hand when it's time to assemble the tamales.

Assembling the tamales:

- Place one of the larger banana leaf squares on a flat surface; now take one of the smaller squares and center it on top of the larger square. One square should have the veins in the leaf running horizontally, and the other square should have the veins running vertically.
- In the center of the smaller leaf, place a small fist-sized ball of dough. Into the dough press one piece of pork and one teaspoon of rice, and around this arrange 1 slice of bell pepper, 1 prune, 1 olive, 6 peas, 3 chickpeas, and a slice of carrot (or whatever combination of vegetables you choose).
- Turn the top banana leaf so that one of the corners is at 12 o'clock. Fold the top corner down over the dough, the bottom corner up, first one side in and then the other,

so that all of the points have come together at the center forming a closed package.

- Turn the tamale over so that its folded edges are facing downward; and now repeat the sequence, folding the second banana leaf over the first.
- Repeat the whole process with a second tamale and tie the two tamales together, criss-crossing the twine like you were putting a ribbon on a package. Tie the tamales firmly. Two tamales tied together are known as a *piña*.
- Once all the piñas have been made, place them in a large pot and fill it with water. Cover the tamales with any leftover banana leaves and boil them for about 3 hours (remember that the meat was raw when you put it in.)
- Important: If any of the banana leaves are torn during the wrapping process, it is very important to replace them because any tears in the wrapping will allow the water in during steaming and ruin the dough.
- The traditional way to serve tamales is to put them on a plate, cut the strings that bind them, and serve them atop their banana-leaf wrappers.

Note: Tamales store well when frozen. It is not recommended that you reheat them in the oven or microwave; instead leave the tamales in their wrappers and heat in boiling water.

Tamales

Tamales have their origin in the cuisine of the Aztecs, but tamale recipes of many kinds are today an important part of the food culture in Mexico, Central America, and beyond. In Costa Rica, tamales consist of a specially prepared corn masa, or dough, stuffed with beans, pork, or other savory fillings. They are cooked in banana leaves, which impart a unique flavor to the dish.

There are a number of steps in the preparation of tamales. You begin by preparing the corn masa, and then you make the filling. Next, the banana leaves for wrapping the tamales must be cleaned, thoroughly. Finally the tamales are assembled and cooked.

Making tamales is neither fast nor easy. This is why homemade tamales are only prepared at Christmas—although they are available in some restaurants and supermarkets throughout the year. Preparing Christmas tamales is very much a family affair. Mom, children, aunts, and uncles gather on the designated day to divide up the work—and the opportunity to spend time with family is really half the fun of making tamales.

It's not unusal for a single family to make 500 or more tamales; it's customary to offer friends and families a tamal or two as a very personal kind of gift, for, afterall, everyone claims that their mom or grandmother makes the best recipe. The good thing about tamales is that they maintain their taste even when frozen, so that people can enjoy eating them long after the holidays are over.

Specialties

Caribe

Cocadas

(6 - 8 servings)

These tasty little cakes, from the province of Limón, have a pastry base that is topped with grated coconut.

Ingredients:

- ½ cup (1 stick) of butter.
- ¼ cup of sugar.
- 1 cup flour.
- 2 cups grated coconut.
- 1 can of condensed milk (14 oz.).

Preparation:

- Cream the butter and sugar. Add in the flour and continue creaming until the mixture takes on a smooth texture.
- Grease a square ovenproof glass dish (about 8" wide). Pour the mixture into the dish and spread it evenly with your hand (flour your hand first so that it doesn't stick to the dough). Use a spatula to raise the edges up about ⅓ of an inch.
- Evenly spread the grated coconut over the pastry and pour the condensed milk on top. Bake on medium heat for about 30 minutes or until a golden color.
- Remove from the oven, allow to cool, and cut into squares.

Pan Bon

(makes one loaf)

This recipe for pan bon, which is a sweet, dark bread, is one of the signature dishes from the Caribbean province of Limón. (The Afro-Caribbean population of Limón is descended from Jamaican immigrants who arrived to Costa Rica in the 19th century, when Jamaica was still a British colony.)

Ingredients:

- 1 envelope of yeast.
- 2 ½ cups flour.
- 10 oz. (½ block) of tapa de dulce (or 1 ½ cups of brown sugar).
- ½ cup (1 stick) butter, melted.
- 1 cup of a mild, white cheese, grated.
- ½ tablespoon of ground cinnamon.
- ½ tablespoon of vanilla.

bread. Allow the bread to soak up the broth, then mash it up thoroughly. Remove from heat and set aside.
- Mince the garlic, celery, basil, bell pepper, onion, oregano, parsley, and cilantro in a food processor.
- In a another pot (over medium heat), melt the achiote in the oil, and then add the beef, Worcester sauce, and thyme. Continue cooking and stirring until beef is cooked through. Next, add in the ingredients from the food processor.
- Cover the pot and allow it to simmer over medium heat for 10 minutes. Add the mashed bread and the whole hot chili and cook for another 10 minutes, stirring occasionally.
- Remove the chili and the thyme sprig. The final mixture should be fairly thick.

Preparing the pastry:

- Preheat the oven to medium.
- Over medium heat, melt the achiote with 3 tablespoons of shortening. Remove the mixture from the heat and place it in a deep bowl. Mix in the flour and salt.
- Cut up what remains of the shortening into small bits and mix it in. Using a potato masher (or your fingers), mash up the ingredients until the mixture resembles crumbs. Pour in the cold water and knead the dough just until smooth—and then shape it into a ball.
- Use a rolling pin to roll out the dough thinly, but be careful not to tear it. Use a cookie cutter or a glass to cut 4-inch circles out of the dough. Scoop one teaspoon of filling into the center of each circle. Fold the circles in half, using a fork to seal the edges and prick the center.
- Move the patties to a greased ovenproof glass dish and bake until golden brown.
- Serve hot.

Plantain Tarts / Plantintá

(20 - 25 tarts)

A plantain tart is a kind of stuffed pastry that is similar to patí, except with a sweet plantain stuffing.

Ingredients:

- patí pastry dough (see recipe on page 130).
- 2 ripe plantains.
- ½ cup sugar.
- juice of half a lime.
- ½ teaspoon of ground cinnamon.
- 1 drop of red food coloring.

Preparation:

- The dough is the same as that for patí.
- To make the filling, preheat the oven to medium and bake the plantains (without peeling them). When they

are tender, remove them from the oven, peel them, and mash them. Add in the other ingredients and mix well.
- Preheat the oven to medium.
- Just as in the preceding recipe, mix and roll out the dough, and cut, fill, and bake the pastries.

Rice-and-Beans

(6 servings)

This is the signature dish of the province of Limón, whose Afro-Caribbean people use the English name for the delicacy. Rica-and-beans is sometimes described as "the gallo pinto of Limón" since both dishes contain rice and beans. The difference in taste is notable, however, as rice-and-beans contains coconut milk, an ingredient that in Costa Rica appears only in Caribbean-coast cuisine.

Ingredients:

- 3 coconuts, or 3 cups of canned unsweetened coconut milk.
- 3 cups of hot water for the coconut milk (if using fresh coconuts).
- 6 cups of water for the beans.
- ½ cup dried red beans.
- 1 ½ red bell peppers, finely chopped.
- 1 sprig of thyme.
- 3 cups rice.
- salt and pepper (to taste).
- 1 ripe panameño, habanero, or other small hot chili, whole.

Preparation:

- Break open the coconuts and remove the white coconut meat. In order to more easily remove the coconut meat, you can either bake the broken shells in a hot oven for 10 to15 minutes or freeze the coconuts for a couple of hours, until the coconut meat begins to come away from the shell.
- Grate the coconut meat. Combine the grated coconut from a single coconut with 1 cup of hot water and purée in a blender or food processor. Repeat the process for the other two coconuts. Let the blended coconut and water stand for a few minutes and then strain to extract the coconut milk. (Or, you can also use canned coconut milk.)
- Place half of the coconut milk and 6 cups of water in a pot; add in the beans, bell pepper, and thyme. Mix well. Cook over medium heat until the beans are tender (about 1-1 ½ hours).
- When the beans are cooked, add to the pot the rest of the coconut milk, along with the rice, salt, and pepper. Stir well.
- And in the whole chili, reduce heat to low, and cover the pot.
- Cook for approximately 30-45 minutes, or until the rice is done.
- Remove the chili and serve the rice-and-beans hot. This is usually presented as a side dish to either chicken or beef.

Run-down / Rondón

(6 servings)

It has been suggested that this coconut-milk stew came to be called "run-down" because it was made with whatever one could literally run down. Some people make the dish with beef, pork, chicken, or, back in the old days, turtle. But the most popular version of *rondón* (as it came to be known in Spanish) is made with fish.

Ingredients:

- 2 lbs. of fish filets (preferably red snapper), cut into chunks or strips.
- vegetable oil.
- 1 lb. of yuca.
- ½ of a medium breadfruit.
- 5 unripe bananas.
- 6 cups of coconut milk.
- 1 medium onion, chopped.
- 1 stalk of celery, chopped.
- 2 sprigs of thyme.
- ½ teaspoon of pepper.
- salt (to taste).

Preparation:

- Add a dash of vegetable oil to a pan and fry the fish filets until cooked through. Set aside.
- Peel the yuca, the breadfruit, and the bananas, and cut them into chunks. Place them in a pot with the coconut milk and bring to a boil. When the milk starts to curdle

and the fruits are tender, add in the fried fish, onion, celery, thyme, pepper, and salt.
- Continue cooking over medium heat until the mixture thickens.
- Serve hot with white rice or rice-and-beans (see recipe on p. 133).

Note: You can also add other vegetables such as sweet potatoes, plantains, or tiquisque (a tuber.)

Limón Cuisine

Limón, one of Costa Rica's seven provinces, runs along the length of the Caribbean coast. It has a distinct, rich identity that is reflected in its culture, language, festivities, architecture, and, of course, cuisine.

This province has the largest number of Afro-Costa Rican peoples within the country. The first black inhabitants were

African slaves brought over by the Spaniards to work on cocoa platations during the colonial era, but the largest group arrived in the 19th century, after the abolition of slavery. They were mostly Jamaicans—but also immigrants from other Caribbean countries—who came to build the railroad from the Central Valley to the Atlantic port of Limón and to work on the banana plantations.

The new arrivals brought with them their culinary traditions and foods. These new influences mixed with Spanish cuisine, with the foods of the indigenous population, and with the culinary traditions introduced to Costa Rica by immigrants from China and other countries. The result is the colorful and varied cuisine of Limón province that you find today.

The Jamaicans also brought with them their language. This is the origin of the creole English still spoken by many people in Limón, and it explains why the names of certain dishes are in English (like rice-and-beans) or derived from English (like rondón).

A Note on the Ingredients

Below is a description of some of the most commonly used cooking ingredients in Costa Rica. While many of these are readily available worldwide, there are a few that might be hard to come by outside of Central America. If substitute ingredients exist, we indicate those.

Achiote. A small tree or shrub from the tropical regions of the Americas. Its ground seeds (which contain annatto) are used as an almost flavorless coloring for meat and vegetables; it is commonly sold as a paste that has a characteristic red hue.

Arracache. The root of a large-leafed tropical plant. It has something of the texture of a potato, but with less flavor. There is really no substitute.

Ayote. A type of squash. An acceptable substitute might be a winter squash like butternut or cushaw squash.

Breadfruit. Although originally from Southeast Asia, breadfruit has become a staple food in many other tropical regions. In Costa Rica, it is mostly used in dishes made by people living along the Caribbean coast of the country. There is really no substitute for breadfruit, but in the recipe for *rondón*, you can dispense with the breadfruit without dramatically altering the taste of the dish.

Chayote. Also known as *chocho*, *mirliton*, and custard marrow, *chayote* is a pear-shaped fruit (although for all culinary purposes it should be treated as a vegetable) of the *Sechium edule* plant. A proper substitute may be hard to come by outside of Latin America, but zucchini can be used to obtain tasty results in recipes that require *chayote*.

Chorizo. Costa Rican *chorizo* is a type of pork sausage found throughout the country, and is often eaten fried in *gallos* or used to make more elaborate recipes. Any pork sausage is an acceptable substitute.

Complete Seasoning. A popular brand of spice mix in Costa Rica. You can substitute with any mix of dried spices such as *Herbes de Provence*.

Kola Roja Syrup. This is a store product available in Costa Rica; it's pretty much the same thing as Grenadine, which is available worldwide.

Masa. Of a different consistency than corn meal, this prepared corn flour is used to make tortillas, as well as several desserts. Two common brands are Maseca and Masa Rica.

Pejibaye. The fruit of a palm tree species. This was an important food source for the indigenous residents of Central America since before the arrival of the Spaniards, and it remains very popular in Costa Rica today. It has a beautiful red-orange color, a nutty flavor, and a very dry texture. There is really no acceptable substitute.

Queso Blanco. A kind of white cheese that is extremely popular throughout Costa Rica. Use any mild, white cheese as a substitute.

Tapa de Dulce. Meaning "sweet lid," *tapa de dulce* is a dried, unrefined, and unbleached whole sugarcane loaf, also known as *panela* or *piloncillo* in other Latin American countries. In Costa Rica, it is readily available in nearly all supermarkets. If you are unable to find *tapa de dulce*, use an equivalent amount of dark brown sugar instead.

Yuca. Also known as cassava, yuca is the edible root of a woody shrub that is widely cultivated throughout tropical and subtropical regions. Because of its unique consistency and flavor, there is no adequate substitute for it. In recipes where it is not featured prominently (such as *olla de carne* or tripe soup) you can simply leave it out.